# Head and Glory

# Head and Glory

## Sacred Order
### or
### Secular Chaos

## Charles F. Caldwell

Preservation Press, Inc.

P.O. Box 612 • Swedesboro, NJ  08085

Unless otherwise noted, Scriptural quotations are from or based upon the
*Revised Standard Version of the Bible*, © 1946, 1952, 1971, 1973.


Typesetting and Cover Design: Jim Whitacre

**Library of Congress Cataloging-in-Publication Data**

Caldwell, Charles F. (Charles Francis), 1935–
 Head and glory : sacred order or secular chaos / Charles F. Caldwell.
   p.   cm.
 Includes bibliographical references.
 ISBN 1-886412-04-9 (pbk.)
 1. Ordination.  2. Ordination of women.  3. Trinity.  I. Title.
BV664.5.C35  1996
262'.14 –dc20
                                                           96-29118
                                                              CIP

1  2  3  4  5  6  7  8  9  10  Printing/Year  00  99  98  97  96

# DEDICATION

*For*
*Peter, Vita and Deborah Toon,*

*in appreciation and with affection.*

# TABLE OF CONTENTS

*Preface* ............................................................... 9

Introduction ....................................................... 11

**PART I** — THE APOSTOLIC MINISTRY
   I. Institution ................................................. 19
   II. Prophetic Sign ......................................... 25
   III. The Sacrament of Order ......................... 33

**PART II** — IDEOLOGY AND THEOLOGY
   IV. Ideology .................................................. 39
   V. Theology .................................................. 45
   VI. The Dignity of Persons .......................... 51
   VII. Men and Women ................................... 57
   VIII. Apostles and Disciples ......................... 65
   IX. Decently and in Order ........................... 75

**PART III** — SYMBOLIC PERSONS
   X. Ordination ............................................... 87
   XI. Creation, Sin and Salvation ................... 103

*Epilogue* .......................................................... 115
Appendix I — The Trinity and the Blessed Virgin Mary ......... 121
Appendix II — The Trinity and Homosexuality ................... 123
Appendix III — *Ordinatio Sacerdotalis* ....................... 127
Notes ................................................................. 133
Select Bibliography ........................................... 139

# Preface

The first major draft of this book was completed in June 1994 when I was on the faculty of Nashotah House, an Episcopal Seminary in Wisconsin. Sherri Baker was responsible for the word processing and initial sub-editing. I thank her for doing this and other tasks for me.

The final version has been prepared by my good friend, the Rev'd Dr. Peter Toon, a former colleague, and President of the Prayer Book Society of the Episcopal Church. The two of us have cooperated in many ways and I am delighted he has a part in the book. Further, I have dedicated it to him and his family.

After I took early retirement from Nashotah House in July 1995, I suffered a stroke following heart surgery. My recovery has been slow but sure, and I continue to make progress.

I am most grateful to faithful friends who have made it possible to get my manuscript published through their gifts to the Prayer Book Society for this project. Further, it is a pleasure to know that my work is published by Preservation Press. In 1994, I loaned my combined BCP/KJV to Norma and Jim Whitacre, which they used to prepare the edition published by Preservation Press.

The topic of the book is not a popular one in the main-line denominations today! I hope, however, that it will serve the cause of biblical truth in the work of the Kingdom of God.

*Feast of the Ascension, 1996.*
*Charles F. Caldwell*
*Naples, Florida.*

# Introduction

The title of this book, *Head and Glory*, is inspired by St. Paul's teaching, as it was given to the church in Corinth. In fact, it is from a part of the First Letter to Corinth which modern Christians tend to shun or reject!

## APOSTLE OF THE LORD JESUS CHRIST

Apparently few today in the western Church are moved to praise, magnify and adore the Blessed, Holy and Undivided Trinity by what they read in I Corinthians 11:2-16. Seemingly only a minority reads these verses and finds them to be a window opening up to them the vista of the kingdom of God, of divine order in creation and redemption, and of principles to guide the Church today.

Regrettably, by what he wrote here, St. Paul, apostle to the Gentiles, is perceived by many (including a great number who have only glanced at the actual content) as reflecting the worst tendences of the Judaism of his time, revealing himself to be an advocate of "patriarchalism, sexism and androcentricism." In short, it is said that Paul was "against women" and so unlike Jesus, who was all for inclusivity and the equality of women with men!

11

Since we shall have occasion to refer to this passage at different points in this book, let us begin by carefully noting what the apostle actually wrote concerning men and women in Christ.

> I commend you because you remember me in everything and maintain the traditions even as I have delivered them to you. But I want you to understand that the head of every man is Christ, the head of a woman is her husband, and the head of Christ is God [the Father]. Any man who prays or prophesies with his head covered dishonors his head, but any woman who prays or prophesies with her head unveiled dishonors her head—it is the same as if her head were shaven. For if a woman will not veil herself, then she should cut off her hair; but if it is disgraceful for a women to be shorn or shaven, let her wear a veil. For a man ought not to cover his head, since he is the image and glory of God: but woman is the glory of man. (For man was not made from woman, but woman from man.) That is why a women ought to have a veil on her head, because of the angels. (Nevertheless, in the Lord woman is not independent of man nor man of woman; for as woman was made from man, so man is now born of woman. And all things are from God.) Judge for yourselves; is it proper for a woman to pray to God with her head uncovered? Does not nature itself teach you that for a man to wear long hair is degrading to him, but if a woman has long hair, it is her pride? For her hair is given to her for a covering. If any one is disposed to be contentious, we recognize no other practice, nor do the churches of God. (I Cor. 11:2-16)

We may note that Paul's teaching here begins with the confession of the God and Father of our Lord Jesus Christ, the incarnate

Son, who is the Head not only of the Church but of the human race. Into this doctrine of Incarnation, Salvation and Headship there is integrated the doctrine of Creation (from Gen. 1-3). In all the churches of God, the apostle desires to see divine order manifested and upheld for the glory of God.

In looking at this passage, we perhaps need to search for the principles before allowing ourselves to be put off by the outworking of them within a given place and time (long hair, veils etc.—see further Chapter Eight and Chapter Nine, "Apostles and Disciples"). Obviously, St. Paul was addressing Christian Jews and Gentiles in the multi-ethnic, multi-cultural, and polytheistic port city of Corinth! Yet he was also speaking the word of the exalted Lord Jesus, Head of the Church! In this book, we shall search for the principles of divine order in creation and redemption and we shall look for the word of the Lord Jesus, who is the same yesterday, today and forever.

## AN OVERVIEW OF THE CONTENT

"If god is male, the male is god."[1] This statement may not make clear logical sense; but, it does make a certain psychological sense within the disordered passions of many men and women, who suffer from the demons of pride and envy, or from feelings of inferiority and superiority. For, in a world where male and female are considered exclusive categories of difference, complementary opposites, or accidental qualities of human or divine being, to say that god is male is to exclude half of the human and divine reality from consideration as being of true importance.

Such an attitude distorts our behavior as well as our thinking and feeling. It also disorders our interpersonal and social relations as well as our passions.

Since religion is an important cultural influence, it is proposed by some that we should move "beyond God the Father" by ordaining women to the official ministries of the churches. Such action may be thought of as a simple matter of civil and ecclesiastical rights or equal justice under law. Further, it may be explained as a matter of discipline and worship, which does not require a change in doctrine; or it may be understood as a way of changing the symbolic system and therefore the doctrinal structure of the church.

In a culture shaped by a notion of liberty which says that we are free to do as we want, so long as we do not harm others or violate their rights, a negative proof is sometimes given for or against the ordination of women. The issue is thus framed in terms of asking or answering the question, "Why not do it?" On the one hand, it is said that, in the context of the modern definition of theology, there is no valid theological reason against the ordination of women. On the other hand, it is said that, according to traditional theology, the Church has no authority to change the tradition given by Christ's example.

The negative way of putting and discussing the issue usually means that scholarship sets itself the task of either deconstructing or defending the authority of the historical tradition. Theological reasons which might rationalize and justify the proposed changes in the discipline of the Church and the doctrine of God are easily found; but theological reasons for only ordaining men are not always so apparent, and therefore the significance of the tradition is not so clearly rationalized and justified.

This book will investigate the theological reasons for the reservation of ordination to men. It is hoped that its content will be a contribution to the ongoing discussion, and an aid in clarifying an orthodox response to the issues raised by the current movement towards disciplinary and doctrinal revision.

The *first* part is an attempt to distinguish order, office, and ministry, as a way of clarifying the discussion about ordination. Ordination may be considered as an effectual sacramental sign of grace, but the ordained person may also be considered as an effectual sacramental sign of order. In such "order" there is both primacy and equality. The male may be taken as the natural sign of primacy given by God in creation, in the commandments of the law, and in the gospel of salvation, according to Christ's institution.

In modern culture, both conservative and progressive ideologies tend to oppose "law and order" to "freedom and equality." Thus it is not always easy for us to hold together the notions of primacy and equality, in a way which correlates with order and subordination between apostle and disciple, priest and people, men and women, according to the word of the one God who creates, commands, and saves.

Therefore, the *second* part of the book considers conservative, progressive, and moderate ideologies, as systems of meaning and value which influence our behavior, thinking and feeling, and are distinct from a theology oriented towards the knowledge and love of God through his Word.

The Christian understanding of God given by his Word implies both equality and subordination among the Persons of the Trinity. We glorify the Father, and the Son, and the Holy Spirit, and we also pray to the Father, through his only-begotten Son, and with the Holy Spirit. There is communion and an order of relations among the Persons of the Trinity. The Trinitarian principles of monarchy, patriarchy and hierarchy require both order and equality. These principles contrast with modern notions of democracy, bureaucracy, and autocracy, which involve power and dominion.

The biblical, orthodox doctrine of the Trinity has enabled Christians to assert the dignity of persons, as well as the reality of individuals. The distinction between "persons" and "individuals" may be used to discuss the relations between men and women, priest and people, apostle and disciple in terms of primacy and equality. Further, the kinds of order which follow from the principles of monarchy, patriarchy, and hierarchy can help us understand how all things in the Church can be done "decently and in order," without violating our concerns for the values of law and order, or equality and freedom.

The *third* part of the book considers various arguments for and against the ordination of women, given by ancient, medieval, and modern authors. These arguments seem to be based on different notions of ordination as either an order, or an office, or a ministry.

Those ordained are considered to be symbolic persons, somehow representing God, Christ, and the general order of things, as creatures related to one another and to God. Therefore, theological issues for our understanding of God are involved in whether ordination is reserved for men or is open to both men and women.

Finally, the symbolic differences which might arise from thinking of God as "he," "she," or "it," and the doctrines of creation, sin, and salvation are presented according to the principles of monarchy, matriarchy, and patriarchy. The Judeo-Christian doctrine of God as King and Father, who creates, rules and saves by his Word and Spirit, is seen as a basis for understanding the dignity of persons, made for friendship with God and a destiny beyond the boundaries of culture, nature, or history in the resurrection of the dead to eternal life.

# PART ONE

# THE
# APOSTOLIC MINISTRY

# CHAPTER ONE

# Institution

C hrist's institution of the apostolic ministry is variously described in the Four Gospels, but all seem to agree that the calling and sending of the apostles is essential to the proclamation of the good news itself. The apostles were sent into the world after the resurrection of Christ, but they were called to follow and learn of Christ at the very beginning of his ministry, after his baptism by John.[1] They were sent out on mission to prepare the way for Christ's coming, as he journeyed through the country; they were given private instruction with prayer before Christ's passion; and they were commissioned by Christ after his resurrection.

The different accounts of Christ's establishment of the apostolic ministry function in a variety of ways in the theological narrative of the gospel writers as they interpret the meaning of the history of Christ. The institution of the apostolic ministry may have been established by degrees, as in a later age one might think of degrees of advancement in the ordination process. That is, the apostles were initiated into the mystery of Christ by degrees as they were associated with Jesus' prophetic ministry of preaching the kingdom, the priestly ministry of Christ's passion, and the royal ministry of the risen Lord.

## OSTOLIC MINISTRY ESTABLISHED

seems to underlie the various accounts in which ... may be said to have established or instituted the apostolic ministry.[2] That structure may be said to express an apostolic order and a ministerial office. Jesus called and sent, he gave and commanded.

> And he called the twelve together and gave them power and authority over all demons and to cure diseases, and he sent them out to preach the kingdom of God and to heal. And he said to them, "Take nothing for your journey. . . ." (Luke 9:1-3)

> Jesus said to them again, "Peace be with you. As the Father has sent me, even so send I you." And when he had said this, he breathed on them, and said to them, "Receive the Holy Spirit. If you forgive the sins of any, they are forgiven: if you retain the sins of any, they are retained." (John 20:21-23)

There is an order in, through, and by which Christ calls his disciples to follow, imitate, and learn of him, so that they can become like him. Not all of those in the crowds which follow Jesus are called by him to follow him in the master-disciple relationship by which he promises to make them "fishers of men." From among those who have been called to follow Christ, some are chosen and sent as apostles to go before him into the world or into the villages and towns which he himself is to visit. They are effectively to represent him so that "whosoever receives you, receives me, and whosoever receives me receives him who sent me" (Luke 9:48; Luke 10:16; Matt. 10:10). They are sent to do as he does.

As the Father sent Christ into the world and remains with him, so Christ sends the apostles into the villages and towns of all the world and yet remains with them (Matt. 28:16-20). As Christ is from God and for us, the apostles are from Christ and for us—(II Cor. 5:18-20). The calling and sending of the apostles establishes an ordered relation, as they are sent from someone to someone.

Since the apostles are sent to do what Christ does, they are given the authority and power for the work of that office, and they are commanded by Christ concerning that ministerial work. The office and ministry are ordered by their relation to Christ and the world. The apostles are to do the works of Christ on behalf of the world. The shape of the work is determined by the commission and command of Christ, and the ability to do the work is determined by the gift of Christ.

An officer holds delegated authority, power, and responsibility. The officer is responsible to someone for something, and therefore is given the means by which to exercise that responsibility. Authority and power are delegated from someone to another. In the last analysis, Jesus is said to give the apostles the authority and power of the Holy Spirit of God. Jesus gives the apostles the same Spirit whom the Father has given to him. Yet, the Spirit given to Jesus does not cease to be the Holy Spirit of the Father, as the authority and power given by Jesus do not cease to be his own, even when delegated to the apostles.

Such a delegation of the Spirit of God is necessary if the apostles are to do as Christ does, as the Father does, and as Christ commands. He commands them to teach and preach, but his teaching and preaching is with power and authority by which people are liberated and healed. Therefore, when Jesus sends the apostles to preach the gospel of the kingdom, he gives them authority and power to exorcise demons and heal the sick. Such things are signs of who Jesus is and what he has come to do through his Passion and Resurrection—delivering us from the powers of Satan, sin and death, and restore us to everlasting life. He also commands his apostles to baptize (with water and the Holy Spirit) and make eucharist (which he declares to be his own Body and Blood). Further, he commands them to bind and loose according to the law of God and for the cure of souls. Finally, he commands his apostles to forgive and retain sins with the authority and power of the Spirit of God, who makes alive and raises from the dead.

When we consider the shape of the apostolic ministry commanded by Christ, we can perhaps see that the gift of Christ must accompany the exercise of that ministry. For that ministry is not simply a social role or official function in a society thought of as a community of believers, a community of the baptized, or a community of disciples. The Church is not simply a democratic people's republic, in which the apostles are elected and appointed by the disciples. It is an ordered community, in which the apostles are sent to make disciples. In fact, the Church is a communion which includes the saints in heaven and on earth, so that what the apostles bind or loose on earth is also bound or loosed in heaven.

## ORDER, OFFICE AND MINISTRY

Christ's institution of the apostolic ministry indicates that we might profitably distinguish between order, office and ministry. Christ called and sent, he gave and commanded. There is an order of relations, by which Christ calls disciples from the world to follow him, and by which disciples are sent by Christ into the world. There is an office, by which Christ delegates authority, power and responsibility, by the giving of the Spirit he has received from the Father. There is a ministry of service to others in the world, according to Christ's command.

The distinction between office and ministry arises from the notion that one can have authority, power, and responsibility without always exercising it. For instance, one could be a physician with the skills, means and concern for healing, but in the absence of someone who is ill one would not in fact practice medicine. Likewise, one might be equipped as a preacher or teacher, but not exercise those ministries unless there were someone who needed to hear and learn the gospel of Christ. The order of the apostolic ministry (from someone to someone) requires that the apostolic gifts be exercised as ministry for the sake of those to whom one is sent.

It may be said that the notion of "order" indicates a relation, "office" indicates a responsibility, and "ministry" indicates a function. The preaching ministry is a function of service involving those who proclaim and those who hear the proclamation. It is responsible to Christ for the proclamation of the gospel in the world. It is sent by Christ effectually to represent him to others.

Discussions of the institution and nature of the apostolic ministry are often made difficult by a confusion among the notions of order, office, and ministry. Further, the focus of theological reflection on the Christian or apostolic priesthood has tended to shift over the centuries.

The ancient fathers tend to focus on a priesthood of ordered relations, the medieval scholastics tend to focus on a priesthood of official responsibilities, and the moderns of the Reformation and Enlightenment tend to focus on a priesthood of ministerial function. A modern catechism[3] may distinguish the orders and offices of bishops, presbyters, deacons and laity according to a variety of ministerial roles and functions in the faith community. A medieval theologian such as Thomas Aquinas[4] may distinguish the seven major and minor orders according to their rank and official responsibility for the priestly office of offering the Mass as a propiatory sacrifice for the living and dead.

Ancient fathers, such as the author of the *Apostolic Constitutions*[5], may speak of the priesthood in terms of the ordered relations indicated in the law of creation and the gospel of salvation. Scripture and the ancient fathers assert that all things are to be done "decently and in order" (I Cor. 14:40), Thomas Aquinas will suppose that "order is a kind of office,"[6] and moderns seem to assume that office is a kind of ministry.

In order to think clearly and coherently concerning the "ordained ministry" and "ministerial priesthood," we need carefully to ponder the differences and similarities between Order, Office and Ministry.

# CHAPTER TWO

# Prophetic Sign

Why does Jesus institute the apostolic ministry of order and office by calling and sending, giving and commanding? In some sense he may be said to be extending his own ministry and founding a church. But how is this to be understood? Does Jesus train and then send into the field an elite guard for a revolutionary movement of liberation to establish the kingdom of God? Does he appoint officers for a corporation which because of its structure and organization will bear his name and be called "the Body of Christ"?

It would seem that Jesus himself indicated the significance of the apostolic ministry by choosing twelve apostles and then seventy others. Although the names of the twelve vary somewhat in different accounts, the number twelve itself seems to be of great significance, such that after the defection of Judas, Matthias was chosen by the eleven remaining apostles to fill up the number of the twelve (Acts 1:15-26).

All of Jesus' words and deeds can be considered as signs of who he is and what he has come to do. Like the words and symbolic acts of the prophets, they are "prophetic signs" which do what they say and say what they do, because they are signs of the Word of God. The Word of God, spoken by the Spirit of God through the words of the prophets, is effectual, a means both of doing and saying (cf. Is. 55:10-11; Heb. 4:12; Luke 8:11ff.).

## ONE, TWELVE, SEVENTY

The number twelve has a significance in the Scriptures which indicates what Jesus is saying and doing by instituting the apostolic ministry. In the Gospel according to St. Luke, Jesus chooses the twelve and then the seventy. In the Book of Numbers, Moses chooses the twelve heads of the twelve tribes, and then the seventy elders, who are to share his spirit and ministry of judgment (Num. 1; 11:16-30). This numerical pattern of the One, the Twelve, and the Seventy may remind us of the one man, Israel, who went down into Egypt with his twelve sons and their families—(Ex. 1:5). By choosing the Twelve and the Seventy, Jesus is indicating that he is the new Moses and the new Israel. Israel went down into Egypt as a family and came out of Egypt as a federation of tribes, and was reconstituted by Moses as a nation. Jesus is reconstituting Israel in himself with his apostles and elders.

Neither the old nor the new Israel is simply a mob or community of people; they are both ordered communities. They have both order and office. The name "Israel" can be given to the one man, Jacob, and to all those who are associated with him or follow from him through marriage or birth. "Israel" is a man, a family, a confederation of tribes, and a nation. There is an order of birth and begetting from generation to generation and even within a generation, which is indicated by the term "elder." Some are older and some are younger. From among the older and more experienced members of the clan, some are chosen to form a council of elders who can give judgments and make decisions wisely.

The clans may be gathered together as tribes of families having a common ancestor and therefore organized under a "head." In appointing "heads" of tribes and "elders" for the whole nation of Israel, Moses orders the people according to principles of "patriarchy." The twelve sons of Israel are the patriarchs of the twelve tribes which Moses reconstitutes as a single nation. The sons of Israel themselves become fathers, according to an order of generation.

The heads and elders of the people are also officers of the people. That is to say, they have a work or ministry to do. The seventy are chosen by Moses from among those who are "elders of the people and officers over them." They share with Moses in his work of judgment as a prophet of God. They share in what might be called a hierarchical as well as a patriarchal order. The term "patriarchy" refers to the principle of the father, and the term "hierarchy" refers to the principle of that which is holy in the sense of belonging to God.

The elders are given by God a share of the Spirit given to Moses, so that they can share with Moses the burden of judging the people according to the Spirit of God. There is a patriarchal order of elders related to the original father, and there is a hierarchical order of office and ministry anointed by God. The seventy elders represent the principle of patriarchy, inasmuch as they are "elders and officers." They represent the principle of hierarchy, inasmuch as their appointment shows that the Spirit, authority, power, and wisdom of God can be communicated, delegated and shared. These two orders are united in the priestly ministry of Aaron and his sons. Aaron is the brother of Moses and also the prophet who speaks for Moses, as Moses is the prophet who speaks for God (Ex. 4:10-17). The priesthood is given to Aaron and his sons of the tribe of Levi, and it is also a service dedicated to God.

Jesus does not simply call and send apostles, elders and officers, but he also gives them a share in his own Spirit, authority and power for godly ministry. He is quick to assert the difference between the rule and authority of ordinary elders and officers, who exercise dominion over people in the name of the common good, and the apostolic order of godly service (Matt. 20:20-28; Luke 22:24-27). After all, the Spirit and authority of God does not cease to be God's even when it is given to men, as is indicated by the story that the seventy elders appointed by Moses received the Spirit and then prophesied once only, and that Eldad and Medad also prophesied, even though they had remained in the camp, away from the tabernacle. The Spirit was given and rested upon them all, but could not be claimed as their own apart from God and Moses, his prophet (Num. 11:26-30).

There is considerable significance to the numbers One, Twelve, and Seventy when we think of Jesus with those who, according to Luke/Acts, will become his apostles and elders; and Moses, with the twelve heads of the twelve tribes and the seventy elders for the whole nation of Israel; and Jacob or Israel with his twelve sons (the patriarchs of the twelve tribes) and the family of seventy which went down into Egypt.

Moses reconstituted the nation of Israel, a reconstitution for the sake of the nations of the world, fulfilling the destiny and promise of Israel to be a light and blessing to the nations. Israel itself has a larger significance in the cosmic order of things. As there are several ways of naming the apostles to make up the number twelve, so there are various ways of naming the patriarchs to indicate that they are to be thought of as being twelve in number.

Jacob himself, representing the principle of monarchy (the principle of the one in relation to the many; here, the one father who is the father of the fathers), is renamed to indicate his relation to God. He is Israel, the one who has wrestled with God and is mighty with God. And Israel, with his twelve sons and seventy persons, corresponds in some way to the one, the twelve and the seventy which may be seen in the heavens.

The one sun may be thought of as going through the twelve heavenly signs of the zodiac; and in the night sky one may note the seven lights which wander from a fixed path (the sun, the moon and the five ordinarily visible planets, not counting the earth on which one stands). There are seven days in the week made by combining the cycles of the sun and moon. The seventh or Sabbath day is commanded to be kept as a memorial of creation and redemption (Ex. 20:8-11; Deut. 5:12-15). The number "seventy" may be taken to refer to the number of the family of Israel and the number of the nations and their angels which are the "sons of God."[1]

## THE FAMILY OF MAN

If Moses and Jesus Christ reconstitute the nation and family of Israel, Israel itself has a cosmic significance as a reconstitution of the family of Man, who is made in the image and for the likeness of God, to have dominion over the animals of the earth as God has dominion over the gods of heaven. This family is constituted as Adam (the Man), Eve (the Mother of all the Living), and the children by whom they multiply themselves, fill the earth and subdue it. Their destiny for dominion and likeness to God is fulfilled in the Son of Adam (Man) who ascends in the clouds of heaven to the right hand of the throne of God to rule in a kingdom which has no end.[2]

After the fall, new beginnings for mankind were attempted with Noah and Abraham. But Noah (the first man of a new generation of men after the flood) himself sinned, when the previous wicked generation had been destroyed (Gen. 9:20ff). Abraham, chosen from among the nations generated after Noah, followed the call of God to the promised land, but found that his faith and hope failed him, when he was commanded to go into Egypt to multiply under the protection of Pharaoh so as to become a great nation which could take and possess the promised land (Gen. 12:14ff). God reordered things so that the last should be first: Jacob, the second twin, inherited the blessing and birthright of Esau, the first-born (Gen. 27); and the younger son, Joseph, was the first into Egypt and became ruler under Pharaoh (Gen. 37). The order of creation is saved and the disorder of sin is corrected when the order of the world is reversed so that the first shall be last and the last first.

The children of Adam and Eve are both male and female, sons and daughters. "Man" is constituted not as mother (or parents) and children, but as male and female, man and woman. The order of generation from the woman has its beginning in the man. When "the two become one" in coitus, the man cleaves to the woman and gives to her out of himself, so that she may be the mother of living children out of herself. In the process of generation there is an order, from the man to the woman, and then to the children, who themselves are to become men and women, since already they are male and female.

This order of generation may be contrasted with the order of domination which follows the fall and the disordering of creation. According to Genesis 2-3, the woman is in some sense "of the same being" with the Man: "bone of my bone and flesh of my flesh." And so a man "sanctifies" a woman to himself by giving her a gift: a ring or piece of money, coitus, or a written declaration of marriage.[3]

According to a Roman myth, bandits along the Tiber River wanted to found a city, and so they attacked the Sabines and carried off their women. The relations between men and women for the Romans seem to be founded upon rape. The man takes the woman to himself, not by the giving and receiving of a gift, but by carrying the woman over the threshold of his house, feeding her with cake baked in his hearth, and taking her to his bed. The Romans tried to make a correction for the coercion involved in their myth by asserting that marriage was a "matrimony," a law for the protection of mothers, and could not be entered into without free consent. Therefore, a marriage could not be mutually and freely contracted between a master and slave, but only between free citizens. This mutuality of free consent became the basis for the Enlightenment view that marriage is a social contract between free individuals who are basically unrelated except "in-law."

Despite the modern myth that mankind is constituted by individual free human beings who make social contracts with one another, we remain male and female, man and woman, related to one another through birth and marriage by the order of nature created by God and disordered by our fall into sin.

According to the Hebrew Bible, there is a cosmic scheme of things which includes the gods (angels), men, and animals. And there is an order of things which includes men, women, and children. Both the scheme and the order are created by God. In the creation account in Genesis, by believing the snake and acting independently of the man, the woman opens up an opportunity to disorder the scheme of things. But the fall does not occur until the man eats of the forbidden fruit. Prior to that, they were "naked and unashamed," but afterwards they were ashamed and hid themselves. The disorder happened when the man followed the woman. There is order when the woman follows the man, sharing in his life and work in the garden of God.

At the fall, the man followed the suggestion of the woman, and the woman followed the suggestion of the animal, and both ignored God. It was in Adam that all, who follow from him and after him, may be said to sin and die. (Perhaps Adam could have reminded Eve of the commandment, or called her to repentance. If she had remained unrepentant, perhaps God could have made a new woman out of the side of Adam. It is interesting to note that there is an ancient story that Adam had another wife named Lilith.)

Man is primarily responsible before God for keeping the law of God, though the woman is equally responsible. Therefore Psalm 1:1 speaks of the man who keeps the law, and the law itself requires the redemption of the first-born son and is generally addressed to the man. Man, considered as a male animal made in the image of God, and considered as man in relation to woman, is at the root of the problem of sin. Therefore, to correct the disorder of sin, the law is addressed to the man, and the Saviour comes as a man. Jesus is the second Adam; all who follow from him and after him inherit life rather than death. Further, according to some ancient fathers, Mary and the Church are to be considered a second Eve, sharing in the life and work of Christ.

31

# CHAPTER THREE

# The Sacrament of Order

The considerations advanced in Chapter 2 indicate that there is an order in creation, in the law, and in salvation. The same God creates, commands, and saves. The Rabbis note that the same Word of God gives the ten words of creation and the ten words of the law. The Evangelist notes that this same Word, who is spoken by the law and the prophets and the sages, himself has become flesh to speak and live among us (John 1:1ff).

The prophetic signs instituted by Christ, the Word made flesh, include a natural sign taken from the created order, as well as a prophetic word interpreting the sign in relation to salvation in Christ. The apostles baptize with water and the Spirit, washing disciples "in the name of the Father and of the Son and of the Holy Spirit." The eucharist is made with bread and wine, which, according to Christ's command, are said to be his Body and Blood. Healing or exorcism is done with a word, a touch, or oil and with the authority and power of Christ. The sacrament may be said to be an effectual sign which uses both "form" and "matter" with the "motion" of the Spirit and according to the purpose or "end" of Christ.

## DECENTLY AND IN ORDER

There is a relation of order between apostles and disciples, priests and people, men and women, given by the one God who creates, commands and saves. The order in creation and in the law is fulfilled in the order of salvation. In this order, there seems to be a certain primacy and equality, but in any case men are taken as the natural sign of primacy of order.

The ordered relation between apostle and disciple reconstitutes, reorders, and fulfills that relation in the law between priest and people, which in turn signifies a reconstituting, reordering and fulfilling of the natural created order between men and women. This scheme and order of things seems to follow the principles of monarchy, patriarchy and hierarchy.

The members of the *hierarchy* are to live and act according to the principle of the Spirit of holiness who has been given them. The Jerusalem Council of apostles and elders can say, "It seemed good to the Holy Spirit and to us," and Paul can indicate that his priestly ministry is done according to the Word and Spirit of the Father (Acts 15:28; Rom. 15:16). Like *patriarchs*, who can do as their father did, the apostles bestow the Spirit given them by Christ, making both disciples and apostles (Acts 8:14-24; Matt. 28:19). As in a *monarchy*, they follow the principle of the one. Jesus is the one who calls and sends the apostles. Peter is the first to be called and is in some sense the head of the apostles, but this does not mean that Peter is the Chief Executive Officer in a bureaucratic organization, or even the leader who commands obedience. Peter goes off to be first apostle to the Jews of the dispersion, and Paul goes off to be first apostle to the Gentiles. James becomes the head of the apostles and elders at Jerusalem.

At first the apostles travel, preaching the gospel and establishing local churches for which they ordain elders. Bishops come to represent the principle of the one (monarchy) in local area-churches which include many elders, deacons and lay ministers. But the bishops, as overseers, retain something of the general concern for all the churches which characterized the apostles (II Cor. 11:28).

The whole three-fold ministry of bishops, presbyters/priests, and deacons can be thought of as both a local ministry and also as a succession from the apostles instituted by Christ, who called and sent, gave and commanded, according to an order fulfilling the scheme of things given by God. The terms "apostle," "elder" and "minister"(deacon) seem to indicate not a particular office, function, ministry, or role, but a set of ordered relations. The apostle is sent from someone to someone; the elder follows after someone and goes before someone (as in the case of parents and children, older and younger siblings); the minister serves someone on behalf of someone else.

The apostolic ministry of apostles, elders and servers may be said to be instituted by Christ to fulfill his good plan and as an effectual sign or sacrament of order. Men are chosen to signify primacy of order and show that the order of salvation and the order of the law follow the plan and order of creation, according to the purposes of the one living and true God, who is Lord both of nature and grace. However, St. Paul's command that all things be done "decently and in order" is not easy for many moderns to interpret.

## MISUNDERSTANDING ORDER

This is because when we think of order, we are likely to think of the order of a police state, or the order by which we are told to "police" the grounds to neaten them and clean them up, according to the bureaucratic notion that there should be "a place for everything and everything in its place." Every thing should be put in its bureau drawer, according to a preconceived and fixed arrangement. We are likely to think of the "orders" of a dictator, boss, or military commander, who bids us act without thinking, with a kind of blind obedience. As in the schematic order symbolized by a set of bureau drawers, we are likely to think of some in this ordered scheme of things as being larger or smaller than others, on top or beneath others in a scheme of meanings and values.

Thus St. Paul's notion of "decently and in order" may be interpreted according to notions of "law and order" shaped by visions of dictators such as Hitler or Stalin, or mechanical dehumanizing schemes such as some industrial production lines. Of course, in practice we may be for or against having a place for everyone and being able to put everyone in his or her place.

The point is that when we think of order, we do not necessarily first think of the Jewish SDR (Seder), the "Order" of prayer, the Order of Service for Daily Morning and Evening Prayer or the Order for Holy Communion. In an order, there is a first, middle and last; there is a beginning, a means and an end. One thing is first and another is last; one thing follows and leads into another. First this is done, and then that, and afterwards the service is finished.

However, even an order of service may seem confining to some, whose political culture teaches them to value "freedom and equality" over "law and order." Therefore, it may be useful to examine the political ideologies of the left and the right which can influence our readings of the command of St. Paul, the institution of Jesus, and the Sacrament of Order in the Church. It may further be helpful to distinguish between ideology and theology as a basis for our understanding. To this task we shall turn to the next chapter, which begins Part Two.

# PART TWO

# IDEOLOGY
# AND
# THEOLOGY

# CHAPTER FOUR

# Ideology

Theology and ideology are not the same thing, though each may influence the other. Theology may be understood as the knowledge and love of God through his Word. Christian theology, therefore, is often primarily focused on the dogma of the Holy Trinity. An ideology is a system of meanings and values, and often becomes a justification and rationalization for human behavior.

In our modern revolutionary ideologies we often oppose the values of equality and freedom to the values of law and order, identifying them with left or right wing politics and with progressive or conservative movements. "Tradition, Law, and Order" are thought to be the slogans of a conservative ideology. "Liberty, Equality, and Fraternity" are thought to be the slogans of a progressive ideology. "Life, Liberty, and the Pursuit of Happiness" or "Life, Liberty, and Property" are thought to be the slogans of a left of center or a right of center moderate ideology. The moderate may be thought of by some as a "libertarian," the progressive an "egalitarian," and the conservative a "traditionalist." In their own ways, each of these three sets of values reflects a revolutionary ideology, that is to say an ideology which rationalizes and justifies a revolution.

## THE ENGLISH AND FRENCH REVOLUTIONS

The so-called "Glorious Revolution" of 1688 took place in England following the Civil War, Commonwealth, and Restoration. King Charles I was beheaded in 1649, one hundred years after the first Book of Common Prayer was issued. After Cromwell's republican commonwealth, the kingdom was restored in 1660 with the return of Charles II, who was succeeded by a Roman Catholic, James II, in 1685. However, James was forced to flee the country, and Parliament invited William and Mary over from the Netherlands. Unlike the revolution of 1649, the revolution of 1688 was thought to be a "glorious" or bloodless revolution. It sought to conserve and hold in balance both elements of the most recent revolutionary tradition: the divine right of kings with passive obedience by their subjects, and Parliamentary supremacy. The "Glorious Revolution" kept the king as a matter of tradition, but asserted the rule of Parliamentary law. Parliament was to be supreme, since Parliament had deposed James II and elected William III. The ordinary rule of the country was to be by statute law rather than by royal edict. Further, in order to avoid the leveling aspects of the civil war and the commonwealth, the "orders" of society were retained in Parliament and elsewhere. Although the House of Commons would seek to dominate legislation (especially that concerning taxation), the House of Lords would still consist of lords temporal and spiritual and possess certain real though minimal powers. The traditionally ordered society retained the class distinctions among commoners, nobility, and clergy.

One hundred years later, across the English channel in France a traditionally ordered society was overthrown in the bloody revolution of 1789. The conservative cry of "Tradition, Law and Order" was replaced by a progressive cry for "Liberty, Equality, and Fraternity." Such revolutionary values were thought to rationalize and justify the bloody and official homicide of the revolution. A machine, the guillotine, was invented to expedite the beheadings necessary to establish the revolution. Liberty came to mean that the king must be killed (so that there could be no return to rule by royal edict). Equality came to mean that the nobles must be killed and their property expropriated (so that the commons could be supreme in a republican commonwealth). Fraternity came to mean that the clergy or "fathers-in-God" must be killed (so that all could be brothers and share in the commonwealth). There was to be neither God nor master.

In certain ways the dynamic of the French revolution followed the republican impulse of the earlier English revolution, and also continued into the social, political and cultural revolutions which would follow in the future. Liberty is to be gained by overcoming what rules; equality is gained by overthrowing what is noble; and fraternity is gained by eliminating of the fathers. The revolution attacked the Church and the family as well as the king. Progressive legislation would seek to limit the power of family heads to pass on property to their children, by enacting estate and inheritance taxes.

Any form of the principles of monarchy, patriarchy, and hierarchy would be opposed by some as a way of asserting liberty, equality and fraternity against the institutions of government, family, and church, considered as enemies of the revolution. The revolution would keep evolving, as the desire for a classless society extended the notion of the revolutionary brotherhood to include citizens, slaves, workers, and all men.

Such an extension could be justified by the progressive liberal religious slogan, "The Fatherhood of God and the Brotherhood of Man." However, the revolutionary impulse leads to a desire for solidarity among women as well as men, so that "fraternity" is joined by "sorority," brotherhood by sisterhood, and an attempt is made to overcome the class distinction between them by a celebration of "community." The distinctions of social class are to be overcome by attention to what we have in common, and all are to be understood in terms of their common properties.

## THE AMERICAN REVOLUTION

The American revolution of 1776 was a moderate revolution compared to the "glorious" revolution of 1688 and the "bloody" revolution of 1789. It neither killed nor kept the king, the nobles, and the clergy. Although nobility may have been present in the colonies, there was no aristocracy or established ruling class of nobles, apart from those who might be sent to govern in the name of the British king. And while there were established Churches in several of the colonies, there was no common Church Establishment throughout the colonies. Even the Church of England, as represented in the Americas, was remotely governed by the Bishop of London and had no bishops of its own. The king of England himself was across the waters, where he could neither be arrested nor killed.

The blood shed in the American revolution of 1776 was in fact the blood of a civil war which would erupt in 1861. The notion of equality among a single class of commoners might be assumed, but the notion of fraternity with a class of slaves had yet to be asserted. The Declaration of Independence asserted as a self-evident truth that all men are created equal and are endowed by their Creator with inalienable rights to Life, Liberty, and the Pursuit of Happiness. The Constitution, which replaced the Articles of Confederation, allowed the states to permit slavery, and asserted the duty of government to protect "Life, Liberty, and Property." Both sets of slogans intended to assert the rights of the people against the rights of the king, whose authority is asserted by his power of execution, imprisonment, and the imposition of regulations and taxation. The Boston Tea Party likewise seems to indicate that, in the minds of the revolutionary colonists, the pursuit of happiness has something to do with the free use of property.

It may be claimed that at the one end of the spectrum of liberal ideology there is a conservative interest in law and order, while at the other end there is a progressive interest in liberty and equality.

These values seem opposed, although a liberal-minded person might well strongly assert them all, in different times and circumstances, even though they tend to act contrary to one another in the course of our private and public histories. So the question thus arises: Can both equality and order be held together, as in some sense necessary to one another?

Revolutionary ideologies seem to arise as part of a process of the revision of theology, the degeneration of religion, and the secularization of society. In this process certain theological and religious meanings are changed, and this has given rise to problems in interpreting both the Scriptures of our religion and the constitutional documents of our society. For example, "tradition" has come to refer to the continuity of an historical process, rather than the handing over of a gift. Obedience to law has come to mean submission to the will of a lawgiver, rather than a rational love of the good. Order has come to mean a system of classification in which different classes are ranked and filed in their proper places, rather than a plan with a purpose. Liberty has come to mean an assertion of unilateral rights, rather than the fulfillment of God's plan of creation and redemption. Equality has come to mean a statistical uniformity, rather than a just balance. Fraternity has come to be understood in terms of individualism, communalism, humanism, or nationalism, rather than in terms of those personal and natural relations among men and women by which the family consists of father, mother and children.

## CONCLUSION

In this context, there is both the need and the opportunity to assert that the notions of equality and of order can be established in harmony only if they are related to, and defined in terms of, Christian dogma—that of the Holy Trinity and the Person of Christ.

# CHAPTER FIVE

# Theology

Praying and practicing Christians have a basis for understanding that both primacy and equality, and order and sub-ordination, define our relations. There is an ordered equality of relations between men and women, such that while the woman is subordinate to the man, both men and women are one in Christ and are to be subordinate one to the other.[1] Further, there is an ordered equality between priest and acolyte, such that each may respectfully bow to the other, although the priest is celebrating and the acolyte is serving at the Eucharist. Most importantly, there is an ordered equality of relations among the Persons of the Holy and Undivided Trinity, such that we can pray that equal glory be given to the Father, and to the Son, and to the Holy Spirit, and we can pray to the Father, through the Son, in or by the Holy Spirit. We confess a subordination by which all grace comes from the Father, through the Son, and in the Holy Spirit, as all glory is given to the Father, through the Son, and in the Holy Spirit.

The subordination asserted in our prayers by the phrase, "through Jesus Christ our Lord," ought not to be taken to imply a relation of inequality between the Father and the Son, as if one were somehow inferior or superior to the other. Because of the Arian controversy, the Church has asserted that such texts as "My Father is greater than I" (John 14:28) should not be interpreted to mean that the Son is in any way a lesser or inferior God.

Equality is not something to be grasped or held onto independently of the other, and even brothers are to prefer each other in honor (Phil. 2:6 and Rom. 12:10). The forms of moral courtesy are not an assertion of rights and duties, but a free offering of respect and honor to persons, such that one says "please," "thank you," "forgive me," "hello" and "you are welcome," respecting the other's dignity and freedom to the extent that one is even willing to suffer at the hands of evildoers (Rom. 12-13). Subordination is a fact of nature and an act of courtesy.

## NATURE, RELATION AND ORDER

The dogma of the Trinity proclaimed by the Church in the fourth century indicates that in thinking about God we may consider the notions of nature, relation, and order. We may speak both of identity and difference; there are three different Persons with the same, identical substance, properties, and nature. There are three "whos" and one "what," where the "who" is the subject of predication and action. The Son is "one and the same" being, substance, essence, or property with the Father, though the Father is not the Son and the Son is not the Father—such is the teaching of the Nicene Creed—the Son is *homoousios* with the Father. This was important for Athanasius, who opposed the Arians, because salvation by grace means that we are to be "partakers of the divine nature," having "eternal life," having a "common life" or communion and union with the Father and the Son (I Pet. 1:4; John 1:1-3).

The grace of our Lord Jesus Christ is that he, being rich, became poor, so that by his poverty we might be made rich, and that he, knowing no sin, was made sin for us, that in him we might become the righteousness of God (II Cor 8:9; 5:21). According to Athanasius, this grace is the humbling and exalting, the descent and ascent of Incarnation and Deification, for "the Word of God himself was in man that we might be made God; and he manifested himself by a body that we might receive the idea of the unseen Father; and he endured the insolence of men that we might inherit immortality."[2] (It is important to note that in Theology the term "God" refers to either a communicable nature shared equally by the three Persons, or to the Father who communicates his nature to the Son and the Holy Spirit, and who through Christ, the Incarnate Son, shares that nature with us, so that we may become holy as he is holy.)

As Augustine of Hippo observed, the Persons of the Trinity subsist relatively or are subsistent relations.[3] That is to say, the Father is the Father of the Son, as the Son is the Son of the Father. Father and Son are relational terms, but for the Trinity these relations are constitutive of the Persons and not attributes of the divine nature. It is, perhaps, better to say that the Father is God than to say that God is Father. In the one case the term "Father" could be the attribute of the divine nature, while in the other case the term "God" refers to a nature predicated of a person. God is not simply "fatherly" in relation to human beings or other creatures. God is the Father of our Lord Jesus Christ. He is "the Father" in relation to the "Son." The simple use of the term "God" usually refers to the Father, as first in order of relation to his Son. To say this is to assert the primacy of persons rather than common natures.

This primacy of persons is perhaps more easily seen if we consider that the Persons are subsistent relations of order. They are not "three whos and one what" as if the "whos" were interchangeable (as we might say that Peter, Paul and John are three human beings who are, capable of changing places and playing the same roles). The Persons are defined and distinguished by their relations, and those relations are relations of order by which the Persons subsist. The Father begets the Son in such a way that he can say "all that I am and all that I have is yours without ceasing to be mine." God the Father communicates himself, so that the Son is also called the Word of the Father.

God is the living and true God, and not the dead God of the idolaters or the impersonal force and objective idea of the philosophers and psychologists. The living God communicates himself in Word and Act. A person may be thought of as personally present in his actions, and so God the Father may be thought of as personally present not only in his Word or Son, but also in that Person who proceeds from him and returns to him as his own. The Holy Spirit proceeds from the Father, and is Holy as belonging to the Father and sharing his own holy nature.[4]

The Spirit is a divine Person who "comes" and "bears witness." The Holy Spirit proceeds from the Father alone, but is sent to us from the Father by Christ. A later Orthodox formulation will say that the Spirit "proceeds from the Father and rests in the Son."[5] Perhaps this formulation can help overcome our western Enlightenment tendency to understand the person in terms of subject and predicate, project and object.

## LIKE FATHER, LIKE SON

The Holy Trinity is revealed at the Baptism of Jesus, which is also called the Theophany. A voice from heaven is heard, saying, "Thou art my beloved Son." God is shown to be the Father of his Son, Jesus, who is the Christ anointed with the Holy Spirit, who comes and rests upon him (Mark 1:9-11). It is possible that the Spirit came in the visible form of a dove, thereby reminding us of the story of Noah and the flood. As the waters of the flood receded, the dove sent out by Noah returned to him with an olive leaf indicating that the land had dried and was producing plants again. It returned to rest in the ark. The Spirit who proceeds from the Father to the Son, returns to the Father and then comes to rest on the Son. The Spirit is like breath which proceeds from the Father, fills the Son, and is inbreathed to return to the Father, drawing the Son back to the Father, who has begotten him. Like breath, the Spirit proceeds, fills, returns and then comes to rest. The Father can say to the Son "all that I am and all that I have is yours without ceasing to be mine." And the Son can say, "the life of my Father is in me" (cf. Luke 15:11-32). The Son is begotten of the

Father and "inherits" the property of the Father. The Son is also to be or become "like" the Father.

Like his father, a male child can grow up to be a father, but this process of becoming an adult, like one's parent, does not come about by effort and work. One cannot add a cubit to one's life by being anxious (Matt. 6:27). One grows from a child to being a young man or woman by means of the dynamic process of life which unfolds from within. One may choose how to manage this developmental process, and what sort of man or woman one will be, or what one will do with what one has. One may grow up morally right or wrong, but one cannot avoid the dynamic process of growing up. One may vow to be like or unlike one's father, but the life and even the character of one's father may be discovered not only in the father but in oneself. Not only do we live life, but life lives us, and this life is passed on from generation to generation, with a certain will, power and character of its own. This can be either a blessing or a curse, for the sins as well as the virtues of the fathers are visited upon the children, even to the third and fourth generation (Ex. 34:7; Num. 14:18).

Due to this dynamic and ordered relation between the generations, the human person is more than an individual related to other individuals through a variety of associations. He is not like marbles in a jar, which can only touch and to be touched from the outside. Nor is he to be thought of as an individual "human being," having something essential in common with others, but being unrelated to others in their differences. Nor is he to be thought of as related to others by nationality, through birth from a common tribal ancestor or residence in a common country and culture. (In this case, the nation may share a common life for which the individual is expected to live and die, and the nation may be thought of as only externally associated with other nations on the earth.)

Christians ought to be aware that the dogma of the Trinity can help us develop a doctrine of persons which can overcome the dangers of individualism, humanism and nationalism experienced in the twentieth century. In fact, the dogma of the Trinity can help us formulate a doctrine asserting the dignity of persons, since it was through the dogma of the Trinity that the notion of person and personhood was interpreted and defined for the emerging "western civilization."[6]

# CHAPTER SIX

# The Dignity of Persons

A pparently the word *prosopon* ("person") in Greek, originally had reference to the mask worn by players on the stage. The mask had a little megaphone built into it, through which the actor spoke; and "person" meant something through which one speaks. The same actor could play many roles; hence there could be a distinction between the masking role or appearance, the actor who played and interpreted the role (the "hypocrite") and the actor who stood behind the mask and had a life "off stage," apart from the role with its interpretation.

## PROSOPON AND HYPOSTASIS

The terms "hypostasis" in Greek and "substance" in Latin were used to speak of that which stood behind the appearances of things and acted through them. But such terms could be taken to refer either to the actor interpreting the role, or to the acting subject, considered apart from any particular "role" or appearance, and, as it were, "off-stage." Further, "hypostasis" in the East and "person" in the West later came to be in decrees of Councils, used to refer to the underlying personal subject.

In the Latin West, "substance" came to be contrasted with "accidents," and the term "subsistence" came to refer to that which stands behind and acts through both substance and accidents, through both appearances and reality. At the Council of Chalcedon (451), both "hypostasis" and "prosopon" were used to speak of the one Lord Jesus Christ made known in the two natures—i.e., of Christ coming together in one person and one subsistence, one appearance and one agent. The term "substance" came to be used in the Latin and western translations of the Ecumenical Creed as the equivalent of "ousia," so that "one substance with the Father" means "one and the same property" with the Father.[1]

In more recent times, the term "person" has usually been taken to refer to the characteristics of a "personality" or to the one who has that personality. The personal subject may be contrasted with a predicate which defines and qualifies its nature and characteristics; or the subject may be contrasted with its project and object, with its actions and their intentions. The subject is likened to an active agent who throws a projectile towards an objective target. The modern "turn to the subject" indicates that the "person" is to be considered primarily as an active agent, rather than as a visage which appears to an observer, or as something about which one can speak and make statements of predication. Of course, such a consideration is not new to the modern world, but seems indicated by the use of the term "hyparchon" in Scripture and in later church writings, referring to the underlying primary principle (cf. I Cor. 11:7 and the Orthodox liturgical hymn, "*The Monogenes*").

The personal subject who appears in a facial countenance and speaks through all the masks, on stage or offstage, says something to us. The actor and the "person" can be distinguished from the stage sets and the scenery which appear with the actors to make up the performance. The term "person" comes to have a meaning in law, referring to "one of us." If the actor took off his mask, he would be seen to be "one like us," who continues to speak and act "off-stage" in the play of life. The stage sets can be taken down and left to lie. They do not follow us out of the theater.

How might we distinguish between personal subjects and other kinds of subjects? The philosopher Boethius (d. 524) defined a person as an "individual subsistence of a rational nature." The person is an individual, a "corporation" of body, soul, and spirit, which cannot be divided into parts without destroying it. The person is a subsistence, the underlying "who" which stands behind what something is and what it does. What the person is and does is rational: able to think and speak, measuring the proportion of means and ends. The person has a rational nature, for rationality is not simply an appearance or accident which might come and go. Rationality is essential to the nature with which the person comes to be. It is not merely something he does, but something he is, out of which he acts.

Since persons have a rational nature, they are masters rather than slaves, masters who can act in accordance with what they are, and so master themselves and their world. The human person is one who, because of a rational nature, can make boats to ride the waves of the sea, plow and cultivate the land as a garden, build cities for shelter and fellowship, tame animals, fashion art, and know both a visible and an invisible world, a sensible and an intelligible reality, and thus speak with the gods, who, like men, are also persons.

In more modern parlance, a person can be understood to be a self-conscious subject. The "subject" is understood to be an "individual," and self-consciousness is thought to be the mark of rationality. Here the individual is not thought of in terms of a nature which in some sense is shared with others. The individual is thought of as an autonomous self or subject, conscious of its self and its own internal reflections rather than of a sensible and intelligible external reality. It is not entirely clear whether the self is to be thought of as the conscious subject, or as a transcendental Self which becomes conscious in and through that subject. In any case, the "person" is defined as a subject in terms of its own project and object (its consciousness of its self).

## MONARCHY, PATRIARCHY AND HIERARCHY

It is difficult to define a "who" in terms of something other than "what" it is and "what" it does. It is here that the dogma of the Trinity becomes useful, even in defining what we mean by a human "person." For the Persons of the Trinity are understood to be subsistent relations of order. Precisely as subjects, and not simply in terms of their nature and operations, the three Persons are understood in their relations to each other. Those relations are relations of order, such that in some way the Persons subsist in relation to each other; they come to be and to act in relation to each other; they have their beginning and end in another. This order can be thought of in terms of the principles of monarchy, patriarchy, and hierarchy.

The one God is the Father of his only-begotten Son, whom he sanctifies to himself by the Holy Spirit, who proceeds from the Father alone. The term Christ not only refers to Jesus because of his baptismal anointing with the Holy Spirit, but because, within the interpersonal relations of the Trinity, the Holy Spirit, who proceeds from the Father and belongs to the Father, also rests in the Son. The Son is the "Well-Beloved Son." As was noted earlier, such principles are not to be confused with powers. The dogma of the Trinity may show us that monarchy is not to be confused with democracy, patriarchy is not to be confused with autocracy, and hierarchy is not to be confused with bureaucracy. "-Archy" indicates a principle and "-cracy" indicates a power, as when God is spoken of as "pantocrator," the master of all (Rev. 4:8).

The term "monarchy" refers to the principle of the one and the many. In political government this can refer to the one person who is related to many persons as their king, president, chairperson, or head, through a process of election, appointment, inheritance, or domination. The term "democracy" refers to the power of the people. The issue between aristocracy, democracy, autocracy and bureaucracy concerns who shall be master. In the ancient world, legal recognition as "one like us" might be withheld from foreigners and slaves but extended to contractual associations of citizens, who together formed a single "corporation." The primary relation for understanding the "person" for many modern thinkers is the relation between "master" and "slave," oppressor and oppressed. The master comes to understand what is "in himself" by projecting the role of slave onto another who is "for himself." When he reflects and becomes "self-conscious," he becomes a human being who is both "in and for himself," as one who has achieved self-mastery and can recognize in his former slave one who is at least potentially a self-conscious human being.

For theological reflection upon God's self-revelation, the primary relation is that of father and son, rather than of master and slave. The relation between father and son is to be understood in terms of the credal term *homoousion* (one and the same substance or property) rather than in terms of the political category of mastery. Indeed, the king, the father, or the priest may be first in order, even though he is powerless, old, or in exile. The patriarchs of the Old Testament are not necessarily men of power, even though it is through them that birthright and blessing come.

When Jacob obtains his father's blessing by trickery, the patriarch Isaac is too old and feeble to recognize his son by sight, touch or smell. It is Rebecca, his wife, who is master of the situation and dominates it to the advantage of her favorite son (Gen. 27). Here is a story showing the reversal of order, so that the first might be last and the last first (since Esau rather than Jacob was the firstborn), and it is also a story which shows the difference between order and power. Relations of power do not simply replace relations of order, but seek to reverse them and master such property as comes to us in the order of generations as part of our nature and destiny.

The next chapter, continues our reflection on divine order as to consider specifically the relation of man and woman in God's design and plan for mankind.

# CHAPTER SEVEN

# Men and Women

I f persons may be thought of in terms of "subsistent relations of order," men and women may be thought of as "substantial relations of order." That is to say, those fundamental relations of order which define "who" we are, express themselves both in the way we are "what" we are, and therefore do "what" we do. The accidents and appearances by which we identify men and women, male and female, are signs of a substantial relation of order.

## DIFFERENCE, EQUALITY AND ORDER

The problem of identity and difference regarding persons has been discussed with reference to the doctrine of the Trinity. In some way or other, most would agree that men and women are both "the same" and "different" from one another. It would seem that the differences should not be thought of as accidental differences having a common substance, as if the differences were only culturally determined or were merely accidental specializations of biological functions. The differences go beyond those of biological functioning, since every cell in our bodies is genetically stamped as being male or female or is a variation on this two-fold theme.

We are inherently either male or female, both before and after we are able to function biologically for purposes of procreation.

Even on the sexual level, we may note that there is difference, equality and order. The difference is negatively noted by Freud in the male pride and female envy sometimes found in children who have observed that the boy has a penis and the girl does not. Later on a certain equality may be observed, in the discovery that he has a penis and she has a vagina, and that his penis is not for himself but for her, as her vagina is not for herself but for him. Later on, a certain order may be observed through the discovery that in coitus something is given from the man to the woman, and that in birth someone is given from the woman for the man. In some sense, what comes from the man remains his own, even though it is given to the woman, so that the child of the woman is also the child of the man, who must take responsibility for it as the inheritor of his own property and blessing.

The primary relation of order is not that between mother and child, but that between man and woman. Certainly the woman is the mother of both male and female children, but there is a prior gift from the man, such that we can speak of the man being primary, or precedent in order, and the woman secondary but still equal, in the order of generation. He "sanctifies" the woman to himself by giving her a gift. That gift remains his own, so that he can be said to be first in the order of the patriarchy of generation as well as the hierarchy of marriage. He also represents the principle of monarchy, as being the first in an order from which may come many male and female children, wives, servants, relatives and the like. Due to this order, "man" is an inclusive term, according to that manner of speech in which the first thing in a series can stand for itself and all that follows from or after it, and thus encompasses both men and women in general usage.

Some have thought that this order must necessarily involve the power of mastery, since fathers and mothers are bigger than little children, and in some ways men are bigger or stronger or more aggressive than women. As has been noted with Isaac's wife

Rebecca, this is not always the case, and the woman may find ways of reversing the power roles if not the natural order. We honor our fathers and our mothers not because they are always "honorable" but because they are first in order, and their life is in us, so that we will inevitably follow them. When we are small, we can look up to them and know that one day we will be grown up as they are. When we are grown up, we can observe that in the natural order of things one day we will become old and weak as they are, and die as they will die. This natural order is more fundamental than power relationships of mastery and service.

Our so-called gender (=sexual) differences are signs of an ordered relation, rather than signs that we are different species within the same genus or complementary opposites participating in the same dialectically developing whole. The differences are not such as to separate us into two kinds of being, nor are the oppositions such as to make one or the other of us only partially human (although the ancient Greeks had myths expressing such views).[1] Both men and women are whole and entire. Their differences show that they are related to each other, but those relations do not separate them into different species, warring or complementary opposites, or accidental classifications. They are differences of order, so that all that belongs to the man, also belongs to the woman, and will also belong to the children.

Nonetheless, the various myths of male and female relationships do not arise out of nothing. At first in the developing human consciousness, the differences between boy and girl children may seem to be accidental. They both cry and coo; they must be fed, clothed, played with, and toilet trained. Afterwards, the differences may seem to divide them into two species: he has something which she has not; boys and girls separate into same-sex peer group gangs, or clubs. Later, they are discovered to be complementary opposites, as their sexual organs are found to fit together and they appear to be one body with two backs and two motions in a single operation. Finally, the man is discovered to have given a gift to the woman, by which she produces and gives a gift for the man. In this ordered exchange, what is his does not cease to be his because it is given to her, and the child does not cease to be hers because it is for him and has a life from them both.

The principles of monarchy, patriarchy and hierarchy order those substantial relations by which we subsist as male and female persons. The one man (monarchy) is both husband and father (patriarchy) in an order of marriage and generation (hierarchy).

Moderns trained to think in terms of individualism, humanism or nationalism can often see that the relations between mother and child or parents and children make them in some sense one flesh and one family. They are naturally related to one another, or they are intentionally related to one another through responsibility, caring, and sharing. In some political thinking this natural and intentional relationship is interpreted as a legal or contractual relationship, such that the accidental differences of birth and sex can be put aside for the more substantial requirements of the common good and governmental policy. It has even been supposed to be better to have children raised by state agencies rather than by families. In some political thinking the marriage covenant is already reduced to a legal and contractual relationship, such that families joined in marriage are only to be thought of as having relations "in-law," rather than in nature or grace.

## ONE FLESH

In Scripture, one may be "one flesh" with another, either by marriage or birth. The practical consequences of the creation narratives in Genesis 1, 2 and 3 are played out in the legal regulations of Leviticus 17, 18, and 19. In both the story of Creation and in the provisions of the Holiness Code, there is an order by which things are related to one another and to God.[2] There is an order which includes God, Man and animals, and there is an order which includes man, woman, and children. Both orders are given by the Word of the one God. Animals and Man are made on the same day, but Man is in the image of God to have dominion over the animals and is for the likeness of God to subdue the whole earth. The Man names the animals but finds among them no one like himself; therefore God creates from him the woman who is bone of his bone and flesh of his flesh, so that the two shall be one flesh. According to Leviticus 17 the animals may be slain by man for food, but the life blood must be taken for sacrifice, as a representational equivalent for the life of man, whom God's merciful justice spares by the offering of a life for a life. In Leviticus 19, man is commanded to be like God: "You shall be holy, for I the Lord your God am holy." For the sake of this holiness, man is to love his neighbor as himself, which raises the question of the "self."

In Leviticus 18 there is strong indication that this self is not a single individual of flesh and skin, or body, soul, and spirit. Such an individual is "one flesh" or the "same flesh" with his wife and children. On the natural level one enters into one flesh relations of order by either birth or marriage. To make the distinction, we might say that we can be flesh and skin, flesh and blood, or flesh and bone. Those who are one flesh and bone appear to make up a single articulated body, though they are different persons. Those who are one flesh and blood appear to be a single family, living on from generation to generation. The individual flesh, which is covered with skin, senses and lives a single life-time.

There is a one-flesh relation of order between men and women, parents and children, such that they may be said to be kindred by relations of affinity or consanguinity. In its twentieth century canons, the Episcopal Church in the United States of America only recognized prior relations of consanguinity as impediments to marriage, whereas King Henry VIII of England had argued that he could not properly have married his brother's wife, since they were already "one flesh" through a relation of affinity (Lev. 18:16).[3] The recognition of the relations of affinity provided a test case of morality for Paul, who objected to someone "having his father's wife" (I Cor. 5:1), even though she was not necessarily the man's mother (Lev. 18:7-8). Incest could be either through relations of consanguinity or affinity.

It may be said that the man who loves his wife does not love his neighbor as himself, but loves himself (Eph. 5:28). The rich man, in the parable of Dives and Lazarus, is not commended for turning from selfishness to altruism and a "love of neighbor" when he asks that Lazarus be sent to call Dives' five brothers to repentance. He has not shown love to Lazarus, his neighbor. In loving his brothers, he has not loved his neighbor but himself, as his own flesh lives on in and through his brothers (Luke 16:19-31).

Man is not simply to be understood as an individual, separated from others of the same kind but only touching them externally, like marbles in a jar. The telephone company speaks to the alienated and separated individual of the modern world when it invites its customers to "Reach out and Touch Someone." Such an appeal resonates with modern "polymorphous sensuality," which seeks to evade the essentially procreative nature of avoids the sexual process by divorce, abortion, contraception, and oral, anal, or manual stimulation. There is a profound difference between such sensuality and true sexuality, with its process of courtship, marriage, birth, nurture, age, and death. Sensuality takes many forms, as ways of avoiding and denying both sexuality and death. Sensuality gives rise to a lust for a life of self-centered gratification, and a rage against anything which reminds us that there is a natural standard of righteousness which is intelligible rather than simply sensible (Wisdom of Solomon 1:12-2:24).

Man is not simply a being of flesh and skin which is sensitive to the touch and gives an awareness of pleasure or pain. Man is also a being of flesh and blood, flesh and bone. Both man and woman bear on their own bodies the signs and marks of that personhood by which they have ordered relations with others. We are not like the neuter "Barbie Doll" of popular culture. We have both belly buttons and genitals, signs that we are from someone and for someone. We have a nature which we have received from another, with which we are "naturally" born—the term "nature" refers to that which we have by birth and by which our "coming to be" is formed or directed. The mark of the umbilical cord remains on us for life. We each have a set of genitals which are signs that we are for another. Our happiness and natural destiny are to be found not in ourselves, but in another.

Myths of self-realization, self-fulfillment and self-actualization are myths for the person trapped in polymorphous sensuality. They are myths by which we come to use and abuse others for "love" of an individual "self-consciousness." Such myths are lies which lead us to disordered passions and a disordered society. They are not myths which readily incline us to die for either God, country, friend or neighbor, let alone for our husbands, wives, children and parents.

Many people today fear that the principles of monarchy, patriarchy, and hierarchy are illusions which a false consciousness uses to mask the power-reality of democracy, autocracy, and bureaucracy. They use that fear as a justification and rationalization for a continuing revolution. They base their need to dominate persons and societies on the requirements of an ever-changing industrial/economic process. Political and sexual misbehavior are rationalized and justified by appeals to modern ideology.[4] Such ideologies then become the standards by which Scripture and theology are judged and revised.[5]

Thus, when the Christian Church is blown by the winds of modernity, confusion in doctrine, morality and piety ensues. Often on Sunday mornings a religious vocabulary is being used to express what is, in essence, secular ideology in liturgical dress. Further, what seem to be shepherds are in reality "wolves in sheep's clothing," devouring the faithful.

# CHAPTER EIGHT

# Apostles and Disciples

The person may be thought of as a subsistent relation of order in a rational nature. Male and female may be thought of as substantial relations of order, so that men and women are substantial relations of order in a rational nature. Apostles and disciples may be thought of as sacramental relations of order in Christ. Order follows the same principles in creation and nature, as well as the law and the gospel, for there is one living and true God, and "whatever things come from God have relation of order to each other, and to God himself."[1] The principles of monarchy, patriarchy, and hierarchy are essential not only to the dogma of the Holy Triune God, but also to the Christian understanding of the dignity of persons, salvation in Christ, and the apostolic ministry.

## TRADITION, IMITATION AND COMMUNION

When St. Paul speaks of the ordered relations of apostles and disciples, he speaks in terms of tradition, imitation, and communion. To the Corinthians he says, "Be imitators of me, as I am of Christ. I commend you because you remember me in everything and maintain the traditions even as I have delivered them unto you" (I Cor. 11:1-2).

He then goes on to speak of the orders between men and women and of the disorder in the eucharistic celebration at Corinth. In the previous section of the Epistle, St. Paul has spoken of the eucharist as a sacrifice to God and communion in Christ. Now he speaks of it as a tradition received of the Lord and handed on to the Corinthians, as something instituted by Christ when he was "traditioned" or betrayed, and when he "traditioned" himself by giving the bread and wine as being his body and blood, commanding his apostles to "do this" and imitate him. St. Paul then goes on to develop the idea of the body of Christ filled with the Holy Spirit, ending with the exhortation and command that all things be done "decently and in order" (I Cor. 14:40). Tradition, imitation, and communion are expressions of order. The same principles of order and plan are found not only in the ordered relations between men and women, but also between apostles and disciples.

The patriarchal order between father and son is likewise to be understood in terms of tradition. The father begets the son, and the son inherits from the father. The genealogical lists frequently found in Scripture illustrate the importance of the patriarchal tradition of the generations (e.g., see the lists in I and II Chronicles). In this tradition there is also imitation. According to the natural order of things, the son will grow up to be a father like his father, and will also grow old and die like his fathers.

The relation between master and disciple is also an ordered relation of tradition and imitation. The disciple is not above the master, but every perfect disciple shall be as his master. The disciple watches, remembers and imitates the master, so that he too can learn the discipline which his teacher has mastered. The relation between master and disciple is not that between master and slave. The disciple may begin as a servant and end as a friend, since in serving the master and imitating him, the disciple has learned both to love the master and to love what the master loves. The slave is to do the will of the master without questioning. The disciple learns by asking and answering questions. The disciple and the master come to share the same rational love of the good, the same understanding of the proportion between means and ends.

The goal of the master (and of the father) is that the disciple (and son) should come to be as the master (and father). The purpose of obedience is learning and preparing for an inheritance, not the domination of one person by another. Order does not mean that the master or father wants to keep the disciple or son "in his place" at the feet of the master or as a child in the household. The master or father wants to exalt the disciple or the son to the same place where he himself is. The order of tradition is from someone to someone. The order of imitation is "as . . . so . . . ." As the father or the master is, so shall the son or disciple be.

The ordered relations between men and women begin as relations of tradition and imitation between equals, and are more clearly characterized as symbols of communion, or a common life and property, in which "the two shall become one." In Genesis 2 the woman is portrayed as like the man. She is "bone of his bone and flesh of his flesh," and she is to be a "helpmeet like himself." Unlike the animals, the woman is like the man, for she shares the same life and properties with him. She is to participate in his life and work before God in the garden. Thus the man can say to the woman, "you are mine and all that I have is yours, without ceasing to be mine, so that we two shall be one." That order of union and communion through the giving of a gift is expressed in the ancient English marriage rite, when the man says to the woman: "With this Ring I thee wed, with my body I thee worship, and with all my worldly goods I thee endow: In the Name of the Father, and of the Son, and of the Holy Ghost. Amen."[2]

This order of tradition, imitation, and communion, based on the principles of patriarchy, hierarchy, and monarchy, is found between God and man, as well as between man and woman, and apostle and disciple. For man is made in the image of God, for the sake of likeness to God; man can be called the son of God; and God can be called the bridegroom, husband and "man" who marries Israel and becomes one with mankind.[3] The ordered relation between God and man is mediated by Jesus Christ, the Son of God who is filled with the Spirit of the Father, and who is himself both God and Man. He mediates an order in which the property and life of God is shared with man, but does not cease to be God's.

This relation of order between God and man established through Christ is communicated to the disciples through the apostles: "For all things are yours, whether Paul or Apollos or Cephas or the world or life or death or the present or the future, all are yours; and you are Christ's, and Christ is God's" (I. Cor. 3:21ff). The same order between God and man is expressed in another way, when St. Paul asserts that "the head of every man is Christ, the head of a woman is her husband and the head of Christ is God" (I Cor. 11:3).

The communion of man and woman, where the two have become one flesh, is considered by St. Paul as referring to a single articulated body of flesh and bones. The unity of the body is found in the union of head and body, body and members. The relation between head and body or members is ordered according to the principle of monarchy, and has to do with the relations between the one and the many who follow after it or are in some way related to it.[4] When an army is drawn up in order according to a battle plan, the leading center can be called the head and the two flanks can be called the horns of the bull, while the main body of the army remains in reserve, ready to throw its weight where needed. The head of the bull has horns lowered and is ready for the charge. There is an order and a plan, by which the many act together as one.

In Christ there is a union whereby the many become one. That union is with Christ, who is the Son of God on whom the Spirit rests. The union is for the planned, intentional, and ministerial use of spiritual gifts, according to the operations of the Holy Spirit in the body of the Son. The union is according to an order of relations. "In Christ Jesus you are all sons of God, through faith.

For as many of you as were baptized into Christ have put on Christ. There is neither Jew nor Greek, there is neither slave nor free, there is neither male nor female; for you are all one in Christ Jesus. And if you are Christ's, then you are Abraham's seed, heirs according to promise" (Gal. 3:26-29; cf. Col. 3:11).

In Christ there is union and order; the head of the woman is the man, and Christ is the Son of God who was born of a woman (Gal. 4:4-7). Salvation according to God's promise of grace is to the Jew first and then also to the Gentile Greek, so that even today the "old" testament Scriptures come first before the "new" testament Scriptures which follow after them (Rom. 1:16).

In that union and communion of the one and the many according to the principle of monarchy, there is also a hierarchy by which the many are to be like the one. Christ is the Word of God, the image and likeness of God, and through him all things are made (John 1:1-18; Heb. 1:1-4). Man is made in the image and for the likeness of God, to have dominion on the earth and grow up into heaven. It may also be said that man is made in the likeness and for the image (Gen. 1:26-27, 5:1-4). Man is male and female, not in the sense of complementary opposites making up a whole, but in the sense of significant relations of order. "In the image of God created he him; male and female created he them." Man is both a masculine singular, and a plural which is both male and female. The patriarch has both sons and daughters. The primary relation is therefore between male and female, man and woman.

**IMAGE AND GLORY**

St. Paul speaks of "image and likeness" in terms of "image and glory". The terms "image and likeness" are not simple equivalents for "male and female", for both terms are used of the male. There is a sense in which the woman is related to the man as a likeness, and the man is both in the image and in the likeness of God (Gen. 2:18; 1:27, 5:1). St. Paul seems to bring together several accounts of the creation of Man by speaking in terms of "image and glory." He writes: "(For man) is the image and glory of God; but woman is the glory of the man. For man was not made from woman, but woman from man. Neither was man created for woman, but woman for man... Nevertheless, in the Lord woman is not independent of man nor man of woman; for as woman was made from man, so man is now born of woman. And all things are from God" (I Cor. 11:7-12).

The distinction between an image and a likeness may be indicated by using the Aristotelian categories of "form" and "matter," "motion" and "end." The same form may be in a different matter (as in the case of an icon, or the man who is an animal formed to have dominion over the other animals on earth as God has dominion over the gods in heaven), or the same form may inform another which has the same kind of "material" nature (as in the case of Adam begetting Seth, or Jesus being in the form of God prior to the Incarnation). The same form can be in a fixed image or in a moving image: in an icon or a mirror. Adam is to be the living image of the living God, not like the idols which are dead images of dead gods (cf. Wisdom 13:10-14:31).

Adam is in the image of God in that he is to have dominion, and he is in the likeness of God in that he reproduces his own image. The term "image" may be taken to refer primarily to what man is, and the term "likeness" to what he does. In the order of things man is the living image of God, and woman is the mirror image of man. The same form and indeed the same operation can be communicated from one thing to another in such a way that both are equal and their differences only show their relations of order. The disciple is to be like his master, the woman is to be like the man, and man is to be like God. There is an order in which one follows the other in an operation ordered to a good end. The end of the work of God and man, working together, is man come alive with eternal life in the kingdom of God; the glory of God is the salvation of man.

In addition to headship and communion based on the principle of monarchy, and imitation and likeness based on the principle of hierarchy, there is a tradition and authority based on the principle of patriarchy. Man has a primacy of order such that he may be said to "subsist" as the image and glory of God.[5] Woman may be said to be subordinate but equal, since she has authority from the man (I Cor. 14:34; 11:10). It would seem that "authority" has as little to do with the authenticity of authorship as "hierarchy" has to do with a higher or lower rank. To have authority (*exousia*) is to have a property from another.

Jesus delegates authority to his apostles, so that they have a power and property by which even the demons are subordinate to them. The apostles and elders sent by Christ do not have to perform exorcisms by means of magic rites and incantations. The demons recognize and freely obey the word of the apostolic ministers of Christ. Jesus' ministry with Satan and the demons is not so much a power struggle as it is the reordering of that which had been disordered. Jesus can say to Peter, "Get behind me, Satan," for the proper place of Satan is behind us as a goad to righteousness rather than in front of us as a leader to sin. The issue is over who follows whom. Due to the spirit of authority and power, which is given by Jesus to the apostolic ministers, the demons are freely subordinate to them, as the Corinthians are to be freely subordinate to the first converts in Achaia, as the spirits of the prophets are subordinate to the prophets, and as the women are to be freely subordinate to men (I Cor. 16:15-16; 14:32, 34).

## WOMEN IN CHURCH

In the Church of God, the woman is not to act as if she were an individual separate from or unrelated to either God or men. Nor is she to act as if this relation were not an ordered relation. The symbolic custom of the head covering for women praying and prophesying in the congregation indicates that the woman is not to have the glory of her hair uncovered, as if she were a maiden seeking the courtship of a man, but not yet related to a man by marriage. Nor is she to go about as if her head were shorn and her glory shamed because of a disordering of the relation between man and woman through something like adultery or fornication. She is to cover her head as a way of putting authority on her head, to show that she has property given to her by another to whom she is now related. The married woman has authority and power in the household which is no less than her husband's, precisely because it is given by her husband as a gift ("with my body I thee worship and with all my worldly goods I thee endow"). The authority and power is hers without ceasing to be his.

There is a patriarchal tradition of authority and power from the Father to the Son, from Christ to the apostles and from the man to the woman. In that order, apostle and disciple, priest and people, man and woman are related to one another and to God. The woman is to put a covering on her head to claim her authority and keep apart from the disorder of sin. She is to claim her authority "because of the angels" (I Cor. 11:10).

This reference to the angels may refer to the interpretation of Genesis 6 in the Book of Enoch. The angelic watchers are spoken of as the sons of God who cohabited with the daughters of men. They had been sent to teach man the arts and sciences, so that man would properly fill and subdue the earth after his fall and exile. But the inclination of the angelic gods was to be like men, as the inclination of men was to be like gods (cf. Gen. 3:5). The watchers wanted to be able to multiply and subdue the earth.[6] They taught men the arts and sciences of seduction and war, for they seduced the daughters of men, and the children born of them were giants who made war on earth. When the giants died, their souls were demons, a mixture of the human and the divine in a way fit neither for converse with gods or men. Wickedness increased on the earth, and world empires rose to subdue men themselves.

The disorder of Genesis 2 and 3 can be attributed primarily to the man, although the woman had an equal, if subordinate, part in it. In the Enochian interpretation of Genesis 6, there is a further fall into disorder. The woman does not claim her authority and power from the man or from God. She stands separately from God and man in a disordered relation with the angels. St. Paul's command that the woman should put authority on her head indicates that she should claim her authority and power within the ordered relations of the body of Christ, if sin and disorder are to be avoided.

This order of head and glory, principal and authority, communion, imitation and tradition, according to the principles of monarchy, patriarchy and hierarchy, is according to the "command of the Lord."[7] It is according to creation and nature as well as the law and the gospel. St. Paul appeals to the law of Moses and the creation of God when he discusses the order of headship, glory and authority. He appeals to the natural order as recognized by the customs of the nations when he speaks of shame and honor. He appeals to the order of salvation through the preaching of the gospel when he speaks of the Law, and the word of God which has come from others to the Corinthians (I Cor. 11:3-16; 11:14; 14:34, 36).

What is the command of the Lord to which St. Paul also appeals? This command is not simply a saying of Jesus which we do not find recorded in the gospels (cf. the saying in Acts 20:35). In the institution of the apostolic ministry, by which the apostles are sent and authorized to make disciples, Jesus brings together the orders of creation, the law and the gospel, so that the order of men and women, prophets and people, apostles and disciples becomes a prophetic, sacramental and effectual sign of Christ and his mission. In the light of this institution, St. Paul interprets the supper of the Lord as both a sacrifice and a communion, for the relation of priest and people is like that of men and women (I Cor. 10:16-18). This institution of Christ seems to be a key for understanding his whole mission, for he shows that he has come to fulfill the promise of God in the word of creation and the law, reconstituting Israel and mankind for the sake of the kingdom.

St. Paul indicates that his own insights into the command of Christ are things which must be explained if they are to be understood, but he expects the faithful to recognize the command of the Lord in what he is writing (I Cor. 11:3). It seems that St. Paul is able to recommend a church discipline of "non-recognition" as well as of "excommunication" and "anathema" (Gal 1:9; I Cor. 5:1-5; 14:38). If someone preaches another gospel than that first preached by the apostle, such a person is to be cursed. If someone does not repent of incest he is to be excommunicated. If someone does not recognize the command of the Lord in these writings of his apostle, such a person is not to be recognized as one of the brethren of the apostle.

St. Paul's use of the term "brethren" to address the Corinthians and the Galatians should not be taken in the bureaucratic sense of classification, separation, and ranking which moderns consider sexist and exclusive. "Brothers" is not simply the complementary opposite of "sisters." In the order of relations from the patriarch Adam, all men and women may be considered as brothers and sisters to one another (Tobit 8:4-7). In Christ, the baptized and the faithful are one because all are "sons," inheritors of the promises and property of God in his kingdom (Gal. 3:26). Therefore, in the order of apostles and disciples all may be called "brethren," though some may be elder fathers in God (I Cor. 4:14-16) and brethren in the faith. In Christ, the Church is composed of sons who have God for their Father and the Virgin Mary as their mother (Gal. 4:4, 6; John 19:26, 27), but in relation to Christ the Church is a bride, and the faithful are prepared for baptism as virgins for a marriage (II Cor. 11:2-4). The old Israel, also, may be considered as the son or the betrothed bride of God, and may be spoken of as either "he" or "she" (Hosea 11:1; 2:2, 6, 23).

The key to understanding St. Paul's use of masculine and feminine terms is not one of "opposition" but "order." This is so important that the next chapter is devoted to the explication and development of what "decently and in order" means.

# CHAPTER NINE

# Decently and in Order

How shall we understand St. Paul's exhortation that all things be done "decently and in order," which sums up his concerns in I Corinthians 11-14? St. Thomas observed that there are two kinds of order: that by which creatures are related to one another, and that by which they are related to God. God is the framer of both kinds of order, and in the dogma of the Trinity, God is the monarch who is both patriarch and hierarch, begetting and sanctifying his Son Jesus Christ.

## A SCHEME OF THINGS

There is a created order of kindred relations by birth and marriage, generation and sanctification.[1] There is an order of priest and people in the old covenant, and there is an order of apostle and disciple in the new covenant, both of which fulfill and reconstitute the promise given in the order of men and women. That promise involves both a "scheme of things" which ranks the orders of gods (angels), men, and animals; and it involves an order of men, women, and children. The scheme is part of a plan according to which man is made a little lower than the gods, so that he might be crowned with glory. The angels prepared the Gentiles for the law, and gave the law as a preparation for Christ, who has come that man might be equal with the angels in having eternal life, and higher than the angels in the kingdom of God.[2] This "scheme of things" fulfills the purpose of the order of man, woman, and children, that Man should be fruitful, multiply, fill the earth and subdue it, for the Son of Man rules from heaven in a kingdom without end.

The difference between a "schema" and an "order" may be likened to the difference between rank and file in a military formation. The ranks can be thought of as having a left, right and center, while the files have a first, middle and last. But the positions can be changed if the formation does a left face, a right face or an about face. What was a rank can become a file, and what was first can become last. Both schema and order have to do with relations. St. Paul's exhortation could be translated "let all things be done schematically and according to order," except that he speaks, not only of a scheme but of a "good scheme." The word *euschemonos* (from *euschema*) is often translated as "decently"—as in the Revised Standard Version. However, in contemporary English "decently" can carry a sense of niceness and prettiness, rather than the sense of acting according to an intentional plan. A "good scheme" is a well thought out plan. If an order has a first, middle, and last, a good plan has a beginning, means, and end. To obey the commands of Christ according to a well ordered plan is to share his rational love of the good, to recognize the proportion between means and ends. St. Paul wants the Corinthians not only to seek heavenly spiritual gifts of a high rank, but to covet earnestly the higher gifts—faith, hope and love, being greater gifts than tongues or prophecy.

How, then, might things be ordered in the churches according to a good plan or scheme of things? St. Paul mentions customs which might guide the local congregation in its ordered worship of God. Men are to pray or prophesy with uncovered heads, while women are to cover their heads when praying or prophesying, and to keep silence except when praying or prophesying.

It would appear that women are not to engage in the dialogic arguments about the law and the gospel, in which one answered a question with a question and gave an answer to the first question only after the second question had been answered. There is a logical order of argument which follows the ordered scheme of things and is founded on the Word of God.

For instance, after the sending and return of the seventy, a lawyer asks Jesus, "Teacher, what good thing shall I do to inherit eternal life?" Jesus answers with a question, "What is written in the law? How do you read?" The lawyer answers by quoting the commandments to love God and neighbor (according to the two orders noted by St. Thomas). Jesus then answers the first question according to the answer and understanding shown by the lawyer: "You have answered right; do this and you shall live." The dialogue continues when the lawyer asks a further question which follows from Jesus' answer, "And who is my neighbor?" Jesus replies with a parable designed to make the lawyer think about the law in terms of a particular case. After telling the parable of the good Samaritan, the priest, and the Levite, Jesus asks, "Which of these three, do you think, proved neighbor to the man who fell among robbers?" Thus Jesus answered a question with a question. When the lawyer replied, "The one who showed mercy on him," Jesus indicated that the answer had indeed been drawn out of the student by the teacher, replying "Go and do likewise" (Luke 10:37).

This dialogic order of teaching between master and disciple is not unrelated to the order of preaching and hearing by which the gospel is spread. The lawyer had stood up to put Jesus to the test while Jesus was speaking with the disciples. Afterwards, Jesus resumes his journey, enters a village and is received into the house of a woman named Martha, thus following the pattern outlined at the sending of the seventy. Martha was busy about many things, while her sister Mary "sat at the Lord's feet and listened to his teaching." Martha asks Jesus a question and tells him what to do about it: "Lord, do you not care that my sister has left me to serve alone? Tell her then to help me." Jesus gives a direct reply to her petition: "Martha, Martha, you are anxious and troubled about many things; one thing is needful. Mary has chosen the good portion, which shall not be taken from her" (Luke 10:38-42). There is a logical order of questions and answers, and also of speaking and hearing, and that order must be respected if one is to choose the good portion and do the good thing.

A good scheme or plan has to do with a work to be done for a good end or purpose. In some ways "order and good scheme" are related as are "order and office." The office is for the sake of a work which is done according to the proportion of means and ends, in order that some good may be accomplished. How, then, are the offices of the church to be ordered for the good of God's kingdom and according to the common life and work shared by apostles and disciples? How can primacy and equality be manifested in that common work of the Church which is the service of God? St. Paul speaks of the common and diverse gifts of the Spirit, the service of the Lord and the operations of the one God which are given for the common good (I Cor. 12:4-7). In later times the Church also developed ways of doing things according to a good plan and order, when it considered the work of the Church according to the offices of prophet, priest and king. In the Old Testament, men were anointed as a visible sign that the Spirit of God was given to them for the office and work of a prophet, priest or king.

### PROPHET, PRIEST AND KING

How is the work of *prophet*, *priest* and *king* to be done, with a good schematic and according to the principles of order?

In a sense all of the disciples are *prophets* in speaking the word of God and the gospel of the kingdom (cf. Matt. 5:12). But there is an order which first involves apostles, then prophets, then teachers (I Cor. 12:28), and finally witnesses to Christ and the gospel of God. Perhaps it may be said that, in the common work of proclaiming the word of God, the apostle is primarily responsible for proclaiming the good news of Jesus Christ and the kingdom. As at the day of Pentecost, present experience is interpreted according to the Scriptures, the gospel of Jesus is announced, and the people are exhorted (Acts 2:14-42). The apostles are sent from Christ, but the prophets speak the word of God to people in their present circumstances (Acts 11:28; 21:10). They are not necessarily apostles, but they are co-ministers of Christ with them (Eph. 2:19-20). They can speak for the ascended Christ. Since they call people to repentance and exhort them to "think again," the meaning of the prophecy must be judged and discerned. For instance, St. Paul hears the prophecy of Agabus that he will be imprisoned if he goes to Jerusalem, but he goes anyway. He goes, not blindly but willingly, ready to suffer and serve for the good of the kingdom.

If the word of the apostles and prophets is to be heard, learned and "inwardly digested," so as to bring forth the fruit of good works, the meaning of that word must be taught. That teaching may be by means of questions followed by questions, and answers followed by conclusions, for the sake of understanding, insight and wisdom. The teachers deal with the word of God in law and gospel, given through the apostles and prophets. This ought to lead to a knowledge and understanding of Christ himself (Eph. 4:20). Therefore the disciples of Christ are to become witnesses for Christ. Everyone does not have to preach, prophesy or teach, but all should bear witness to what they have seen and heard of Christ Jesus in the Spirit.

Often unbelievers do not want to come to listen to a sermon, attend a worship service, or enroll in a study class, but they are eager to hear what Jesus has done in the lives of their fellow citizens in the world. No one member of the body has to do the work of the whole, but all are engaged in a common work in order to accomplish a good end. All are equal workers in the office of prophecy given to Christ and his church, but there is an order of primacy and subordination. In one way the apostles are first and the witness is last, but in another way the witnesses are first and the apostles last. The order is from God, the Lord, and the Spirit, "for the life of the world" (John 6:51).

In the office of the *king*, ordered according to the principle of monarchy, the one is ordered to the many, and the many are ordered from the one. Therefore, the king does not rule alone, as a tyrant, dictator or autocrat. The king is one, but he rules and judges with the council of his peers, the advice of his ministers, and the consent of the people. The gifts of the Spirit include wisdom and understanding, council and strength, knowledge and true godliness, and holy fear (Is. 11:2ff). Someone must make the final judgment or decision, but only after hearing the debate, arguments, interpretations and considerations of those who share the responsibility equally with him. What is good and right must also be practical, and so the advice of those ministers who must see that theory is put into practice must be sought. Finally, the people must give consent, showing that they understand and are ready to do, for it is they who must perform the art of proportioning means to ends, plans to purposes, operations to goals.

In some ways such an order and scheme of rule may be like that at the Jerusalem Council of the "apostles and elders with the whole church," where Peter may be said to have held a primacy of order and James a primacy of office (Acts 15). Later in the Church, this order in the royal office would come to include the bishop, the elders, the deacons and the people. The elders provide a council, the bishop makes a judgment, the deacons administer service, and the people give consent. Without the consent of the people a law is invalid, even if proclaimed by a lawful authority. To give free consent, the people must be informed by a rational love of the good. This concern for a good scheme of things is shown in the Jerusalem Council's statement that their decree seemed good to the apostles and elders and to the whole church, as well as to the Holy Spirit. The royal order relates men to one another and to God.

The Church is not only a kingdom, but a *priestly kingdom* with a *royal priesthood* (I Pet. 2:5, 9; Ex. 19:6; Rev. 1:5). The fact that the whole of Israel is a royal priesthood does not mean that there is not an order of *priests* within it, following Moses, his brother Aaron and his sons, the tribe of Levi which was set apart from the other tribes for the service of God, or the sons of Zadok from the days of David the king. Within the Levitical priesthood there was an Aaronic priesthood, and the temple was later given to the Zadokite priesthood, thus distinguishing the worship at the temple from the worship at the old shrines of the northern kingdom. The use of a different priestly order often indicated a different covenant relation with God.

In the new covenant Christ is a priest after the order of Melchezidek, who was the king of Jerusalem who offered sacrifices for Abraham (Heb. 5:6, 10, 6:20, 7:1-21; Ps. 110:4; Gen. 14:18). There is a difference between the priestly order of Aaron and that of Christ.

The apostle Paul thinks of himself as offering a priestly ministry and a liturgical service of God through his preaching of the gospel of Jesus Christ, so that the offering up of the Gentiles might be a reasonable, holy and living sacrifice, being sanctified by the Holy Spirit (Rom. 15:16, 12:1-2; Eph. 5:1-2). The priestly ministry of the apostles is done by speaking the word of God through preaching, prayer and blessing. Even today in the Eucharist, the priest speaks the effectual, living word of Christ when he says "This is my Body" on behalf of Christ in his glorified heavenly body, Christ in his mystical body the Church, and for himself as a priest—thereby effectually making the sacramental body of Christ, which he prays may be offered up and sanctified by the Holy Spirit on behalf of all, as a propitiation pleasing to God and for the good of the living and the dead.

This priestly action of the apostolic ministry is not done alone; it is done according to an ordered scheme. As the people give their consent to the royal decree, so the laity give their consent to the prayers of the priest, saying "Amen." Beyond that, the Church worked out an ordered scheme by which it was manifest that all were involved in a common work before God, according to their several orders.

In the early liturgies it was often the case that the people would pray at the bidding of the deacon, the priestly elder would collect their prayers into a single prayer offered through Christ, and the Bishop would pronounce God's blessing or intercede for the fulfillment of their petitions in a final prayer of "inclination," for which the people bowed down to receive the blessing for which they had asked. The bishop performed the office of a high priest, the presbyter performed the office of a priest, the deacon that of a Levite/servant, and the laity performed the office of the royal priesthood. The deacon would know the various needs for which prayer was required, since he administered the patrimony of the local church. He could announce the intention, bid the people pray or bow the knee in prayer, and bid the people rise. The people could pray silently, they could fill in the outline of the deacon with their own words and thoughts and desires, or together they could make a vocal petition, such as "Lord have mercy." The presbyter/priest could gather these intentions together in a collect prayer, so that the offering of the faithful was a single offering to the Father through Christ and with the Holy Spirit. At the end of this litany-type liturgical service of prayer, the bishop could invoke God's blessing, as the high priest of the Old Covenant blessed the people in the name of God.

These same principles of order may be manifested in different ways today in the local parish church. The liturgical service may have a variety of lay and clerical ministers following an order of service dedicated to the glory of God and the salvation of souls. Even in the so-called non-liturgical churches, there is an order and scheme of things with a first, middle and last, and a beginning, a means and an end. There is an order of prayer and praise, preaching and witnessing, which follows a pattern and plan by which all can cooperate in a common work for a common purpose. Similarly, in the work of prophetic preaching, witnessing may be done by lay people, teaching through a televangelist, prophecy through study and prayer groups in which spiritual insights are shared, and an apostolic doctrinal message provided by the pastoral oversight of the chief minister. The local church may be governed by the chief pastor with a council of governing elders or a vestry, and with the advice and input of administrative boards responsible for a variety of ministries (education, social services, worship, evangelism, etc.) which are themselves in touch with the needs and abilities, opportunities and problems, strengths and weaknesses of various people inside and outside the congregation.

In this order there may be times and places in which the congregation is young and inexperienced. Strong direction and simple teaching may be necessary; the people may need to be fed with milk before they are given meat, and instructed in first principles before they are given more advanced responsibilities (I Cor. 3:2; Heb. 6:1ff). **The goal and purpose of the ordered scheme of governance, preaching, and service is not that the people should be kept in an inferior or dependent position as children, but that they should be enabled to rise to possess an equal weight of glory with those before them in order. Primacy of order is for the sake of equality of property and life in Christ and the Holy Spirit.**

# PART THREE

# SYMBOLIC PERSONS

# CHAPTER TEN

# Ordination

Women can and do serve in a variety of ministries in the ordered offices of prophet, priest, and king. In many ways they have governed, prayed, and taught as representatives of Christ and the Church. However, the issue of having women in the Christian priesthood is not simply a question of precedent or cultural conditioning. It is well known that many of the non-Christian religions which have existed alongside the old and new Israel have had women priests and ministers. Nor is the issue properly framed in terms of whether women are or can be equal with men in status or in the performance of a variety of ministerial services.

**The issue is whether women can be proper natural signs for the Christian sacrament of order.** It may be observed that the arguments for and against women in the priesthood vary in modern, medieval, and ancient times, according to whether ordination is considered to be for a functional ministry, an official rank, or a sacramental sign of order in creation and salvation. Contemporary Anglican and Orthodox arguments for and against women in the priesthood seem to assume that ordination in the Church is to a functional role as a ministerial representative of Jesus Christ. For the Anglicans, this representation may be said to be "exemplary," while for the Orthodox, it is "iconic."

## ANGLICAN—EXEMPLARY REPRESENTATION

The Anglican argument for the ordination of women is stated in the Letter of December 1985 of the Archbishop of Canterbury to Cardinal Willebrands, President of the Vatican Secretariat for Promoting Christian Unity.[1] Archbishop Runcie noted that Anglican Churches which have admitted women to the ordained ministry have not "intended to depart from the traditional understanding of apostolic ministry...," and he wrote:

> Leaving aside sociological and cultural considerations . . . what I consider to be the most substantial theological reason. . . is seen not only to justify the ordination of women . . . but actually to require it . . . .

> Because the humanity of Christ our High Priest includes male and female, it is thus urged that the ministerial priesthood should now be opened to women in order and more perfectly to represent Christ's inclusive High Priesthood.

> This argument makes no judgment upon the past, but is strengthened today by the fact that the representational nature of the ministerial priesthood is actually weakened by a solely male priesthood, when exclusively male leadership has been largely surrendered in many human societies.

Dr. Runcie's point is that both male and female are human, and therefore the representatives of Jesus Christ must be both male and female if they are to perfectly represent his inclusive humanity.

However, according to an argument based on order, which we favor, "man" is the inclusive term, since it also refers to the women and children and all that follows from the one who has primacy.

In contrast, according to an argument—e.g., the Anglican—based on exclusive classifications, male and female are different specifications in a common genus, or complementary opposites which participate in a whole. Male and female are exclusive terms, which are united in a common human quality that is neuter in gender.

The argument based on order can speak of the noun "man", and so refer to a concrete, historical, reality. In contrast, the argument based on exemplary representation of a common generic "humanity" must speak in terms of adjectives rather than nouns. It does not note that the common humanity belongs to "persons," who are not simply "individuals" (individual human beings) but subsistent and substantial relations of order (men and women).

## ORTHODOX—ICONIC REPRESENTATION

The Orthodox argument against the ordination of women is stated by a subcommittee of the Ecumenical Task Force of the Orthodox Church in America in its book *Women and Men in the Church* (1985):

> Bishops and priests in the Church are sacramentally ordained to actualize the presence and power of Jesus himself in the Church, Christ's own personal and individual presence and actuality as the good pastor, the great high priest, the head of the body, the husband of the churchly spouse, the bridegroom of his pure bride. In order for the bishop and priest to complete his sacramental task for the sake of the whole Church, therefore, he must be one who can image, symbolize, and mystically actualize the Lord's presence as husband and father of the flock. It is impossible for a woman to exercise this ministry and fulfill this task.[2]

Whereas, for the modernist neo-Anglican view the priest is an exemplary representative of Christ's inclusive humanity, for the

89

American Orthodox the priest is an icon which actualizes the presence and power of Jesus himself.

Since Christ is male, the icon must represent him as male. His maleness is not an accident, but is the bodily historical form of the Incarnation, as chosen by God for a reason. The male priest is chosen as one who can represent Christ in his masculine relation to the flock as husband and father, head of the body. This view takes seriously the patristic assertion that God did not simply take our common humanity but took a body. It takes seriously the notion that maleness and femaleness are not signs of opposition or exclusion, but signs of relation. However, it does not go on to define that relation as one of order.

## ROMAN CATHOLIC—AN OFFICIAL RANK

In the Roman Catholic view, ordination is called the sacrament of orders, and is restricted to men because the Church is bound by the choice of Christ himself. The Church has no authority to change the institution of Christ.[3] In this view "order" is a kind of class, rank, or office. As the new *Catechism* explains:

> The word *order* in Roman antiquity designated an established civil body, especially a governing body. *Ordinatio* means incorporation into an *ordo*. In the Church there are established bodies which Tradition, not without a basis in Sacred Scripture (cf. Heb 5:6; 7:11; Ps. 110:4), has since ancient times called *taxeis* (Greek) or *ordines*. And so the liturgy speaks of the *ordo episcoporum*, the *ordo presbyterorum*, the *ordo deaconorum*. Other groups also receive this name of *ordo*: catechumens, virgins, spouses, widows, . . .[4]

There is a sense in which both priests and monks can be "in orders." Dionysius, the so-called Pseudo-Aereopagite, indicates in his *Ecclesiastical Hierarchies* that the hierarchy of the Church is

90

composed of monks, clergy and laity. A hierarchy is an ordered plan with a beginning, a means, and an end. The monks show us the way of perfection in the Christian life, the clergy are the means by which we are sanctified for the sake of perfection in holiness, and the laity are those who have begun to follow the way of purification of the passions, which leads through the way of illumination to the perfection of likeness with God in his kingdom. The clergy are similarly ordered according to the way of purification, illumination, and union, into their offices of deacon, priest and bishop. A hierarchy is an ordered operation for the sake of the knowledge of, and likeness to, God.

Religious "orders," therefore, are ways of following Christ in a disciplined manner of life. Both the monk and the clergy follow an ordered way of life, although "religious orders," as a classification, can include both men and women, while the clergy, as a class of people, only includes men. Classes of people can be distinguished by the work that they do, by their "office" in society. In medieval society the clergy could be thought of as the intellectual class which teaches and prays, the nobility were the military class which defended and ruled, the commons were the working class of traders, artisans, farmers and servants.

"Order" may be thought of as a kind of class (a body of people) or as a kind of office (according to the work which distinguishes different bodies of people in society), and officers can be ranked according to their degree of greatness. Some are general officers, responsible for the strategic oversight of an operation; others are commissioned officers, responsible for the tactical direction of the operation, and others are "line officers," responsible for the execution of the operation. Thomas Aquinas argues that order is a kind of office and that the sacrament of order is a sign signifying "eminence of degree."[5] Order, as a way of following comes to mean order as a class, an office, and a degree of rank.

So it is said that a woman cannot validly receive the sacrament of order because she cannot materially signify "eminence of degree."

Certain things are required in the recipient of a sacrament as being required for the validity of the sacrament, and if such things be lacking, one can receive neither the sacrament nor the reality of the sacrament. Other things, however, are required, not for the validity of the sacrament, but for its lawfulness, as being congruous to the sacrament; and without these one receives the sacrament (sign) but not the reality of the sacrament (thing). Accordingly, we must say that the male sex is required for receiving orders not only in the second, but also in the first way. Wherefore even though a woman were made the object of all that is done in conferring orders, she would not receive orders, for since a sacrament is a sign not only the thing (or grace) is necessary to what is undertaken in the sacrament, but the signification of the thing, is required in all sacramental actions... Accordingly, since it is not possible for the female sex to signify eminence of degree, for a woman is in the state of subjection, it follows that she cannot receive the sacrament of order ...[6]

The argument is based on sacramental signification rather than on exemplary or iconic representation. The priesthood is thought of primarily as an office, rather than either as a ministry or an order.

The distinction between order and office can perhaps be seen by noting that orders have equality in a common work, while offices can be ranked according to degrees of eminence. The rector and curate are both in priestly orders, but one has a more eminent degree of rank than the other. The focus on order as a kind of office and rank seems to lead St. Thomas to consider the relation of men and women according to the work which they can do independently of one another or for which their cooperation is required. Following Aristotle, this leads him to consider man to be more noble, while woman is in some way "defective and misbegotten." Subordination is thought of not so much as a free courtesy among equals (as when we say "if you please . . ." and mean it), but as a subjection which is servile, economic, or civil. Subordination may be said to exist between equals; subjection is said to be between a superior and his subjects.

St. Thomas Aquinas explained:

> It was necessary for woman to be made, as the Scripture says, as a helper to man; not, indeed, as a helpmate in other works, as some say, since man can be more efficiently helped by another man in other works; but as a helper in the work of generation... Among perfect animals the active power of generation belongs to the male sex, and the passive power to the female. And as among animals there is a vital operation nobler than generation, to which their life is principally directed; therefore the male sex is not found in continual union with the female in perfect animals, but only at the time of coition; so that we may consider that by this means the male and female are one... But man is yet further ordered to a still nobler vital action, and that is intellectual operation. Therefore, there was a greater reason for the distinction of these two forces in man...
>
> As regards the individual nature, woman is defective and misbegotten, for the active force in the male seed tends to the production of a perfect likeness in the masculine sex; while the production of woman comes from defect in the active force or from some material indisposition, or even from external influence... On the other hand, as regards human nature in general, woman is not misbegotten, but is included in nature's

intention as directed to the work of generation. Now the general intention of nature depends on God, who is the universal author of nature. Therefore, in producing nature, God formed not only the male but also the female.

Subjection is two-fold. One is servile, by virtue of which a superior makes use of a subject for his own benefit; and this kind of subjection began after sin. There is another kind of subjection, which is called economic or civil, where by the superior makes use of his subjects for their own benefit and good; and this kind of subjection existed even before sin. For good order would have been wanting in the human family if some were not governed by others wiser than themselves. So by such a kind of subjection woman is naturally subject to man, because in man the discretion of human reason predominates.[7]

To many Roman Catholics today the teaching of St. Thomas seems harsh and unlikely to be persuasive in the modern world. Thus, contemporary Roman Catholics may combine the concerns of office and ministry by speaking of the priesthood "in the light of the order of creation and redemption" as an "effective representation of the ministry of Christ."[8] Male and female are considered, not in terms of their ordered relations, or their sexual roles and functions in reproduction, but as the symbolic bearers of masculine and feminine qualities. For instance, the ancient astrological symbol for Venus and the feminine is a circle with crossing diameters which mark its center (or the crossed lines may be drawn beneath the circle). This same image of a centered circumference can be used to symbolize the archetypical pattern manifested in the woman, the city and the world. According to Jungian typology it can also symbolize the all-inclusive God who is an image of the transcendental Self.

The ancient astrological symbol for Mars and the masculine is a circle with an arrow or spear coming from the center and projecting out beyond the circumference. This symbolizes a directedness rather than a centeredness. This can symbolize the man, who wants to make war as well as love, who goes on a journey beyond the confines of the home or the city, and who is always taking "one step beyond" in acts of self-transcendence. The feminine image can become a symbol of immanence, while the masculine image becomes a symbol of transcendence. When the original God is thought of as male, this indicates that there is a religion of transcendence. The feminine can therefore be taken as a symbol for creation, while the masculine is taken as a symbol for the transcendent God.

Such a view is helpful in relating our understanding of male and female qualities to our understanding of God and the world, as well as to our understanding of the priesthood as a symbolic representation. However, male and female must also be considered to subsist in ordered relations, as well to have masculine and feminine qualities with symbolic significance. Existing in a set of ordered relations with other nations and with God, Israel is called God's son or God's betrothed bride. God has chosen Israel as his own bride out of the many nations of the world, and God has also brought Israel into existence when it was no nation, so that as a son, Israel could inherit the land and the kingdom of promise. In the end the difference between God and the world, or God and man, is not the difference between complementary opposites such as masculine and feminine, active and passive, transcendent and immanent, or the like. The difference is one of order, in which there is tradition, imitation, and communion. In the end Christ delivers the kingdom to the Father that God may be all in all. Offices such as teaching and learning, begetting and bearing, or even creating and existing, may be complementary works. But, the signs of order are signs of relations of primacy and equality more basic than relations of complementary opposites.

## PATRISTIC—ORDER

In the *Apostolic Constitutions*, a fourth century collection of ecclesiastical law, the argument against women in the priesthood is framed in a way which follows St. Paul's statements to the Corinthians concerning order. The issue which gives rise to an argument about the ordination of women usually seems to concern that ministry by which the church initially meets the world. In the modern world that ministry is often thought of as one of leadership and governance of the flock of Christ, as is shown in the quotations given from the Letter of the Archbishop of Canterbury, the Statement of Ecumenical Task Force of the Orthodox Church in America, and the *Catechism of the Catholic Church* (1994). The Church is presented to the world as a congregation which gathers for worship and disperses into the world for ministry.

In the medieval world the chief manifestation of the Church was not a congregation associated with its leaders for the purpose of preaching, worship and service; the chief manifestation of the Church in society was the cult or divine service by which the propitiatory sacrifice of the Mass was offered for the living and the dead. Therefore St. Thomas Aquinas defines the various degrees of the priesthood according to their relation to the offering of the Mass. By this accounting it is not at all clear that a bishop is in holy orders, since his distinctive office is to govern rather than offer.[9]

In the ancient world it was often the case that baptism was the chief sacrament by which the Church presented itself to the world. The Church was in the business of converting the world. Preaching was public, but the eucharistic sacrifice was a mystery reserved for the baptized faithful. The issue which gave rise to controversy about whether women could properly be ordained to the priesthood was the issue of who could baptize, rather than who could celebrate Mass or who should govern the congregation.

For the writers of the *Apostolic Constitutions* the issue concerning the ordination of women was not so much whether such an action were permitted, justified, required or forbidden; nor was the issue spoken of in terms of validity and whether or not a woman could receive the grace of orders even if she were ordained. Rather, the issue concerned the peril, danger, wickedness and impiety of such actions. It was asserted that it is not advisable or permissible for a woman or one of the laity to perform any of the offices of the priesthood, not so much because they could not do the ministerial work, or even because God would not communicate his grace, nor because simply nothing would happen, but precisely because something might happen and what happened would be "gravely disordered," and thus contrary to the principles of order given by God in creation, providence and salvation.

St. Paul's statements about the woman being the glory of the man who is her head are used to assert that "the man is the head of the woman." This accords with the principles of creation and with the providence of God after the Fall, which says that the man shall rule over the woman (Gen. 3:16; cf. I Tim. 2:8-15). Although the ignorant Gentiles do have women priests, that is not according to the "order and harmony" instituted by God through creation, providence and salvation. The constitution given by Christ and the apostles forbids "women to teach in the Church" on the practical grounds of Christ's example, the apostolic witness and the danger of disorder.[10] Women deaconesses assist in the baptism of women so that there is no necessity that the "women should be seen by the men." The deacon anoints the forehead with oil, then the deaconess anoints the rest of the body, and finally the bishop anoints the head at the "laying on of hands."[11] The ministry of anointing may be done by the woman deaconess, but it must be done according to the principles of order. It is a ministry done out of a kind of necessity, and not the claiming of an official responsibility. In a similar manner, a female nurse might baptize a gravely ill person in the hospital, but should there be a recovery, that person would be brought to the priest to be enrolled, signed, anointed and validated. The rest of the rite of baptism would be accomplished by the officers of the church when the emergency was past.

The ancient argument that a woman may not take on the office and ministry assigned to the priesthood is based on order, as the following piece from *Apostolic Constitutions* demonstrates:

> Now, as to women's baptizing, we let you know that there is no small peril to those that undertake it. Therefore we do not advise you to it; for it is dangerous, or rather wicked and impious. For if the "man be the head of the woman" (I Cor. 11:3), and he be originally ordained for the priesthood, it is not just to abrogate the order of the creation, and leave the principal to come to the extreme part of the body. For the woman is the body of the man, taken from his side, and subject to him, from whom she was separated for the procreation of children. For says he, "he shall rule over thee" (Gen. 3:16). For the principal part of the woman is the man, as being her head. But if in the foregoing constitutions we have not permitted them to teach, how will one allow them, contrary to nature, to perform the office of a priest? For this is one of the ignorant practices of the Gentile atheism, to ordain women priests to the female deities, not one of the constitutions of Christ. For if baptism were to be administered by women, certainly our Lord would have been baptized by his own mother, and not by John; or when he sent us to baptize, he would have sent along with us women also for this purpose. But now he has nowhere, either by constitution or by writing, delivered to us any such thing; as knowing the order of nature, and

the decency of action; as being the Creator of nature, and the Legislator of the constitution.

Neither do we permit the laity to perform any of the offices belonging to the priesthood; as, for instance, neither the sacrifice, nor baptism, nor the laying on of hands, nor the blessing, whether smaller or greater: for "no one taketh this honor to himself, but he that is called of God" (Heb. 5:4). For such sacred offices are conferred by the laying on of hands of the bishop. But a person to whom such an office is not committed, but seizes upon it for himself, he shall undergo the punishment of Uzziah (II Chron. 26).

Nay, further, we do not permit to the rest of the clergy to baptize, as, for instance, neither to readers, nor singers, nor porters, nor ministers, but to the bishops and presbyters alone, yet so that the deacons are to minister to them therein. But those who venture upon it shall undergo the punishment of the companions of Corah (Num 16). We do not permit presbyters to ordain deacons, or deaconesses, or readers, or ministers, or singers, or porters, but only bishops; for this is the ecclesiastical order and harmony.[12]

Arising from this form of reasoning, we can assert that the term "clergy" refers to a class; the terms "prophet," "priest," and "king," refer to offices; the terms "curate," "rector," "archbishop," "metropolitan," refer to ranks; the titles "reverend," "very reverend," "most reverend," "right reverend," refer to degrees of eminence; and the terms "apostle," "presbyter" ("elder") and "deacon" ("servant") refer to relations of order.

Ordination is not simply induction into an office, appointment for a ministry, or introduction into a collegial body. The ordained person does indeed represent Christ, but in a particular way. All the sacraments are sacraments of Christ; Baptism is the sacrament of incorporation into Christ so that one dies and rises with him; Chrismation is the sacrament of anointing with the Holy Spirit who proceeds from the Father and rests in the Son; the Eucharist is the sacrament of the sacrifice and communion in Christ's Body and Blood; Unction and Absolution are the sacraments of Christ's mission to redeem and restore sinners and to raise the dead; Marriage is the sign of the mystery of union and communion between Christ and his Church.

All the faithful "represent" Christ to the world, but ordination is such to the sacrament of order. The ordained is a sign of that order instituted by Christ at creation, in his providence for a fallen world, in his giving of the law and the covenants, and in his sending of the apostles. That order follows the order of the Holy Trinity, for "as the Father sent me, even so send I you." It is an order following the principles of monarchy, patriarchy, and hierarchy.

The other sacraments are not independent of this order, for when done by those in holy orders they are signs of Christ— prophetic and effectual signs of who he is and what he has come to do. In the Eucharist Christ offers himself to the Father for us; he is signified to be both priest and offering, victor and victim. The minister of the sacraments is not simply a consecrated person who has the authority and power effectively to perform certain actions. Such a person might act for a Christ who was absent from this world and only to be found in past history, the heavenly world, or the world to come. The minister of the sacraments acts for a truly present Christ who is "ordered" from God and for us. The male is the natural sign of primacy in this ordered relation of mission.

In his various letters, Ignatius of Antioch speaks of the bishop as being a type of God the Father, the presbyters as being types of the apostolic college of Christ or the angelic council of God, and the deacons as being types of Christ who is the child or servant of

God.[13] In the *Apostolic Constitutions,* the deaconesses are spoken of as related to the deacon as the Holy Spirit is related to Christ, so that the deaconess should do nothing without the deacon.[14] If one were to think of such a typology only in simple representational terms, it might seem that the bishop represented God the Father, the Deacon represented God the Son, and the Deaconess represented God the Holy Spirit, while the presbyters only represented angels and apostles. It is easy for citizens of a democratic republic to think in such a way, since they are familiar with the process of electing and appointing officials who are "representatives" of the people. However, a type is not simply a representative. The typology in Ignatius to refers to types of order which follow the principles of monarchy, patriarchy and hierarchy.

The relation between the bishop and the elders, Christ and the apostles and God and the angels, is a relation between the one and the many according to the principle of monarchy. God, Christ and the bishop rule, speak and operate with a council of "peers." In Christ both angels and men can be called "sons" of God, being gods themselves by the grace of God, having eternal life, being called saints and being partakers of the divine nature by the grace of Christ. The deacons are to be respected as Jesus Christ, who is the servant of God who became a servant for men, and is the Son of God who inherits all that belongs to the Father, thereby acting on behalf of his Father, himself and us who inherit his kingdom.

The Son of God is sanctified by the Spirit of God. That Holy Spirit is manifested in the many spirits given to the angels and saints. That Holy Spirit proceeds from the Father and rests in the Son, and is therefore sent by the Son from the Father into the world to operate in those who have an ordered relation with the Son. The deaconess is related to the deacon in the economy of the Church, as the Holy Spirit is related to Christ in the economy of the Spirit's mission. There is a distinction between the procession of the Spirit and the mission of the Spirit (John 15:26).

In sum, the typology is intended to signify the relations of order among persons, rather than to represent individuals in a symbolic or official manner.

In one way or another, ordination is to the sacrament of order, and those who are ordained are themselves effectual signs of those relations of order instituted in creation and for salvation. The Holy Trinity and the saints in heaven and earth live according to those ordered relations. By respecting the Christian sacrament of order, society may come to respect the proper dignity of persons. Furthermore, the Church, by recapturing the principle and practice of the sacrament of order, will be in a position, through God's grace, to be "the salt of the earth" and "the light of the world." The ordination of women is to be rejected for right reasons, and those reasons arise from the doctrine of order.

# CHAPTER ELEVEN

# Creation, Sin and Salvation

Certainly the ordination of women makes a civil, political, social, familial and ecclesiastical difference. But does it make any theological difference whether or not women are ordained? Is ordination simply a matter of church discipline, or is it also a matter of theology? Does it make a difference for our knowledge and love of God through his Word? Theology must involve more than "faith seeking understanding" of God's revelation, or the "theory and practice" of Christianity, since we are to be brought to the sharing of a likeness with God, whereby we can become the friends of God (cf. II Chron. 20:7; Ex. 33:11; John 15:14ff).

## HE, SHE OR IT

One way or another, the ordained individual is a symbolic person "representing" God and Christ for us. If only males are ordained to the sacrament of order (as in the traditions of the old and new covenants), we tend to speak of God as "he." If only females were ordained, we would probably speak of God as "she." If both males and females are ordained, we may no longer speak of gods and goddesses, men and women, but of a common, generic humanity or divinity which is "it."

What difference does it make if we call the Creator and Saviour "he," "she," or "it?"

It may be noted that God the Creator and Saviour can be spoken of in terms of roles that are neuter in grammatical gender, without any disrespect or suggestion that God is an impersonal quality or force of "divinity." God can be called "Maker" and "Saviour." When we think of the art of making something, we often make use of Aristotle's categories of matter, form, motion and end. For instance, pieces of wood (matter) can be made into a chair (form), which rests on the floor (motion) and is fashioned for the purpose of being sat in (end), even though that purpose may never be realized or the chair may be in fact used for another purpose (as a ladder to be climbed on, or as a weapon in a western movie).

According to Genesis, God formed man in his own image out of the clay of the earth, breathing his Spirit into man so that man becomes a "living soul" and setting man in the garden to "tend and dress it." Man sinned by "breaking" the commandment and falling short of his own nature and destiny, taking for himself what God had prepared to give him in due time. Man fell short of the likeness of God, and therefore distorted his own nature as one made in the image of God. Our Maker saves us by recapitulating all things in himself, going through our developmental stages and being tempted in all things as we are, and getting it right this time, so that he is without sin, even though he was made to be sin for us. By his grace we are predestined to be conformed to the image of the Son of God (Rom. 8:29).

In the so-called Enlightenment of the eighteenth century, the notion of God was revised to provide an alternative to the so-called theism of orthodox Christianity and the atheism of the radical enlightenment. "Deism" presented God as Maker and Judge, without thinking of God as Redeemer or as "intervening" in the natural and historical process. The world could have an existence independent of God, since matter could be thought of as eternal. The universe could be thought of as a machine, wherein God was thought of as an architect or as a kind of "clock-maker." God might wind the world up at the beginning, but the world could run on by itself. Indeed, the skill of the maker was indicated by the independent operation of that which is made. God made living beings who could live freely and independently by themselves, without the need for the grace of the sacraments, the word, or prayer. Perhaps God might take off the back of the watch to oil it occasionally, passing off a miracle or two to keep it running smoothly, but, in general, He is experienced as an absentee landlord. At the end there will be a judgment according to whether or not the universe or the clock has served its maker for a useful purpose. It may be kept (saved) or thrown away (damned). Jesus is sent by God for the salvation of the world only in the sense that he is an example of faith and morals, showing us how to obey the laws of nature which are the laws of the universe and of God.

In the fourth century, St. Gregory Nazianzen, called "the Theologian," noted that the first principle governing the universe can be that of either anarchy, monarchy or polyarchy.[1] Anarchy seems to correlate to "atheism," monarchy to "monotheism" and polyarchy to "polytheism". The notion that the creator is a maker can lead to the notion of providence, in which something is made out of something, or to the notion of polytheism, in which originally there are at least two principles of an eternal matter and the maker and mover of all. At this point we come face to face with the paganism of Hesiod, who recounts the myth that in the beginning mother earth (*Gaia*) was moved by love (*Eros*) to produce heaven (*Ouranos*) out of her depths (*Tartarus*). Why should the One produce the Many? The principle of monarchy must be interpreted. For the Christian, the one God, who is the Maker (a perfect tense rather than a past tense) of heaven and earth, is also the Father. The monarch is a patriarch and a hierarch.

But what difference would it make were the monarch to be a matriarch? Could the polytheism of gods and goddesses who produce by a process of generation with sexual connotations ("father sky and mother earth"), be avoided by speaking of the monarch, rather than of some of the polyarchs, as "she"? In that case the One would bring forth the Man, as a Mother brings forth diverse children. The Maker could be thought of as creating, not out of something else, but out of herself.[2]

## WHAT IS SALVATION?

Matriarchy explains that God created the world out of Godself, that matter comes from *mater* (the mother). This means that in some sense we are all divine (since we are all of the same being with God) and we are all alienated (since we have come out of God as beings from the Being). Salvation is required, not so much because there has been a fall into sin following the creation, as because the creation itself is a kind of "separation from God." There is a sense in which creation is an original blessing and an original curse, as we fall from God into the world of existence. We long to return to the One from whom we came, and be re-united with the divine Being in which we already participate. Spoken of in gender-neutral terms, it is said that god is our beginning and our end, our origin and our destiny, our source and our goal. In a moment of consciousness we drop from the womb to the tomb.

For the Hindu, the goddess Kali is the mother, the provider and the destroyer of all. Jesus can be thought of as a divine avatar, since the divine being can take many forms. He calls us by word and example to remember our end and our beginning, so that we can intentionally participate in the divine being and even now have the qualities of eternal life. In the light of eternal life, goodness, beauty and being, life is worth living, even in the face of death. Unlike the avatars and sages of the east, who may call us to return to the Nirvana of Nothingness, Jesus reminds us that we are divine and can participate in the divine nature, and that here and now we are to "be somebody." Morality may mean respecting the freedom and divine dignity of every (human?) being.

The theme of life as a process of exile and return is also found in Christian Scripture. Adam and Eve are exiled from the garden, and Jesus promised the thief that "this day you will be with me in Paradise." The Jews were exiled into Babylon and returned to Jerusalem. The Israelites went down into Egypt to multiply and then came out of Egypt as a great nation. Indeed, there is a sense in which the Spirit of God can be thought of as the breath of God, which is breathed out and then breathed in, exhaled and inhaled, as when the Spirit of God hovered on the face of the waters at creation or at Jesus' baptism.

But in the Scriptures the story of exile and return is not the same as the story of creation and salvation. The return to the garden of paradise is only a new beginning for those who are to be exalted to the right hand of God in his kingdom. The good mother does not bring forth children so that they can return to the womb from whence they came, but so that they can be exalted to a grown-up place in the world of the father. The good mother does not keep the children in the circle of the home, but continues to expel them from the home to the school and into the adult world. In a sense mother earth is the origin, but our Father in heaven is our goal.

For the Gnostics, we may have to leave mother earth behind if we are to return to a heavenly mother. Matter may be thought of as that which differentiates us from mater (the mother from whom all comes). In the end, it would seem, matter does not really matter. It makes no real difference whether one is an ascetic or a libertine, since what is done in the body does not matter, so long as one's soul is right in its knowledge of the divine being within and beyond us all.

In his hymns to the Great Mother and to King Helios (the sun), the Roman Emperor Julian the Apostate (d. 363) shows the "post-Christian" phenomenon of matriarchal religion. The first principle of the universe is matriarchal and sets limits to the roving tendencies of the universal male god. That which sets limits to and contains all things is God. The sun is the one light for all the visible (sensible) creation, as the king of the gods is the one god for all the invisible (intelligible) creation. Clearly the sun has limits which define its daily and yearly journeys, so that all may see that the roving male is defined, limited or bounded by the encompassing mother, who is to be thought of as the infinite, the eternal, the boundless, the absolute.

## NATURE AND NATURE'S GOD

The so-called Enlightenment of modern times sought somehow to find a "post-Christian" basis for a society not founded on and justified by the religion of the Church. Grace could be replaced by the nature which it had been said to perfect, and revelation could be replaced by the reason it had been said to illuminate. Atheism proposed to set men free, with neither god nor master. But atheism, nihilism and anarchy did not seem to be a good recipe for a civil society, though they were recipes for revolution. Deism sought to allow for a moral law and judgment, given by God and taught by Christ, and still preserve human freedom from any living god or master. The mechanical world of matter in motion provided a moral law without worship.

The pantheists saw something beautiful revealed in nature, and some of them saw matter as a living, self-moved substance in motion. Pantheism said that matter was moved from within rather than from without. The universe was to be thought of as organic rather than mechanical. One might think of mother nature, who brings forth fruitful plants and animals, which then die and return to the earth from which they came. The natural cycle of generation and mortification, life and death, exile and return, generation and regeneration, could be symbolized in the stories of Jesus' death and resurrection. In some sense the resurrection is to eternal life. The cycles of nature seem eternal; they define our temporal, mortal existence. Though we may die, we will live on in the eternal cycles of generation and regeneration by which one thing is transformed into another. Certainly our bodies are subject to this eternal recycling, and perhaps our souls can be made aware of the process. For the truth is that all things are in god ("panentheism") who is eternal, infinite and boundless.

Pantheism in its various forms is able to use the Christian religion to provide symbols for a religion of nature which worships "nature and nature's God." Deism is able to use the Christian religion to provide symbols for the lessons of the moral and natural laws which are played out in history. Both are exemplified by the thinking of industrial capitalism as manifested in the plantation or the factory systems. Matter in motion, whether conceived as a machine or an organism, is a process which brings forth goods and services. The process has a beginning and an end, inasmuch as the universe is wound up and will wind down, raw materials are put in at the beginning of the process and finished products come out at the end. The process can be thought of as having a direction of progress, revolutionary evolution, or growth. It is not at all clear that the process really goes anywhere or has a purpose. In the end, one seems to return to the beginning, the clock winds down, and the living being returns to the earth from which it came.

All things move forward through time in what seems to be one direction, as night and day follow one another in order. Time is limited, however, and has an end in an eternity which itself is the limit of time, as the cycles of birth, growth, decay and death are continued. Does the universe, in the end, go back to the Nothingness or Boundless Being from which it came? Does the process of becoming end with the beings ceasing to be, so that there is nothing but the Being from which all came? If we return to our beginning, what was the point of coming out in the first place? In Pantheism, we are at the end still faced with the problem of Nothingness and Death.

## GOD AS "OUR FATHER" AND MARY AS "OUR MOTHER"

The good mother does not want the children to hang onto her apron strings, nor does she want to smother them with mother love and stuff them back into the safety and peace of her womb. Rather, she pushes them out into the hands of the father who raises them up to see his face and takes them on to share in his world. The psychologist Eric Fromm speaks of the unconditional love of the mother and the conditional love of the father in his *The Art of Loving* (1956). The mother may love the child, no matter what, but the father must place demands upon the child, if the child is to grow up as a mature adult. We know from the social consequences of single parent families that a child should have both a father and a mother. We are rooted in the earth but we reach out to heaven. We want to "grow up" and not simply to "go back." Orthodox and Catholic Christianity proclaims that Christians are all sons in Christ, so that we have God as our Father and the Virgin Mary as our mother. Mary and the Church are historical types of that heavenly archetype which is the "mother of us all" (Gal. 4:26; Rev. 12:1ff).

What is the difference between a mother and a father? Certainly there is a sense in which the man is prior to the woman in the order of generation. He gives her his seed, and that is necessary before she becomes the mother of the living. Perhaps the man could impregnate the woman and then go off on his own business, without "cleaving to" the woman. Either the god of deism or the roving male deity could initiate a process, and then go off to leave it run along on its own. Being and acting like a male does not necessarily make the man a husband to his wife or a father to their children. Alice von Hildebrand, in a taped lecture, points out that the woman "knows" and the man "believes" that "this is my child." The woman can know, by her own experience and by the testimony of witnesses, that this is her child which came out from her womb. The man must take it on faith that he is the only man who could be the father of that child. The woman is the mother of the child through a natural process, but the man must name and claim the child as his own by nature or adoption. The man becomes a father to the child by a personal act. To be a responsible man, he must name and claim the woman and the children as his own, those whom he will bless with his word and with the property of his inheritance. The man not only impregnates the woman, but is to beget the children. He begets, as he marries, by giving his word of faithfulness.

In the story of the garden of Eden, the man names all the animals, but he does not find among them a helpmeet who is like him and can share his life and work. Finally he sees the woman who is to be called Eve, as the "mother of all living." She is one like himself, and so he names both her and himself in relation to her. He is the "Ish" and she is the "Ishah"; he is the man and she is the woman. He names and claims her as his own, to whom he will cleave.

When the Egyptians thought of the creator god as male, they could think of him as bringing forth creatures through the solitary act of masturbation in an attempt to assert male primacy according to the model of matriarchy. For Christianity, God the Father is not simply a male. He is neither a solitary male nor does he have or need a consort, since he does not create the world out of himself or out of a pre-existent matter. God the Father creates the world out of nothing *(ex nihilo)* by his own Word and Spirit. He speaks and it is done. In the image of creation provided by C. S. Lewis, in his *Chronicles of Narnia* series of so-called children's books, God sings the worlds into existence. There is nothing; there is silence; and then the speaker opens his mouth, and there is something which is filled with the resounding glory of the speaker. Both words and things can be thought of as coming forth from the mouth of God (Deut. 8:3; Matt. 4:4).

God does not have to curse us to make us cease to exist, nor can he go off and leave us to exist independently of himself. Our existence is the evidence that he speaks our name and calls us out of nothing into existence. This "nothing" is not a boundless and eternally empty abyss of "something." That is much more like the chaos of primal matter, which has the potential to take any form given it. To say that God created the world out of nothing is to deny that God made the world out of an unformed no-particular-thing, and to deny that God made the world out of Godself. It is to say that God made the world by his Word and Spirit, *ex nihilo*.

By that same Word, God calls us into existence and calls us to himself. He calls our name and says "let there be "N." and there is N. When we forget or do not heed the word which calls us to be, and to become what we are, then we fall away from our own true selves, as well as from the God who calls us to himself in friendship. Sin is a forgetting or a turning away from the word of God, so that we come to believe a lie. First comes the question, "Did God say?"; then comes the lie, "You will not die" (Gen. 3:1-6). That lie plays upon the inclinations of the body, soul and spirit given us by God. Without free obedience to God's word, we die, the glory departs, and we are ashamed.

In the Genesis story of the Fall, the man is no longer the proper head of the woman, the woman is no longer the glory of the man. There is disorder and shame, according to the commentary provided by St. Paul in I Corinthians. Instead of remembering and believing and freely obeying the word of God, now man is to remember that he is dust and to dust he shall return. He has believed a lie and not hoped for glory by the grace of God, and so he has fallen back into the earth from whence he was taken. The story of exile and return is a true story, but it is the story of sin and judgment rather than creation and salvation.

In his *Confessions,* St. Augustine tells us that though he had forgotten God, God had not forgotten him. If we are created and preserved by the Word, we can also be saved by the Word. The Word of God is with God and is God. He spoke at the creation and at the giving of the law; His words were spoken by the Spirit through the prophets; without ceasing to be God he himself also became man, that he might overcome death by death and give eternal life to our bodies, souls and spirits. Our life does move from the womb to the tomb, but we were made by and for God, not for death. The old catechism of *The Book of Common Prayer* (1662) asks, "Why did God make you?"; the answer is, "God made me to know him, to love him, to serve him here on earth, and to be with him forever in heaven."

Salvation comes by the Word of God, who calls us into existence, calls us to himself, and calls us to come forth from the grave. The Word-made-flesh calls out to his dead friend, "Lazarus, come forth!" God creates us out of nothing and saves us by the resurrection of the dead. That is a basic pattern in the gospel story. By the Word of the Lord, heaven and earth are made, the barren conceive, the desert blooms, the Blessed Virgin conceives and becomes a mother while remaining a virgin, the sick are healed, sinners are forgiven and restored, the persecutor is converted, those in darkness see a great light, the weak are made strong, the foolish wise, and the dead are awakened from their sleep. For the Christian, God is never without his Word and Spirit, for the Word is begotten before all worlds, before both time and eternity. For both the Christian and the Jew, God is a God who speaks and it is done.

> Blessed be he who spake, and the world came into existence: blessed be he who was the maker of the world at the beginning: blessed be he who speaketh and doeth; blessed be he who decreeth and performeth: blessed be he who hath mercy upon his creatures: blessed be he who dealeth bountifully with them that reverence him: blessed be he who liveth for ever and endureth to eternity: blessed be he who redeemeth and delivereth: blessed be his Name. Blessed art thou, O Lord our God, King of the universe, O God and merciful Father, praised by the mouth of thy people, lauded and glorified by the tongue of thy pious servants. We also will extol thee, O Lord our God ....[3]

God is the Father and King, the Patriarch and Monarch who speaks and it is done, who creates us out of nothing and saves us by the resurrection from the dead, who names and claims us as his own. "To him be glory in the Church and in Christ Jesus to all generations, for ever and ever. Amen."

# Epilogue

When Christians, influenced by a modern ideology (e.g., "Life, Liberty and the Pursuit of Happiness"), read and interpret the Holy Scriptures, it is common that they can find nothing substantial therein to make them oppose the ordination of women to the presbyterate and episcopate. The ordination of women is seen in one or another way as a question of equal rights and equal opportunity.

However, when Christians, committed to the patristic dogma of the Holy Trinity, read and interpret the Holy Scripture in the light of this orderly teaching, they cannot see how under any possible circumstances the Church could ordain women and do so within the will of God. They have to say with Pope John Paul II: "I declare that the Church has no authority whatsoever to confer priestly ordination on women."

The fact that several Churches, which claim to preserve the apostolic succession of faith and order, have ordained women (e.g., Anglican and Old Catholic) and the further fact that thousands of Roman Catholics in America are pressing for the ordination of women, clearly testifies to the rejection of the principles (found in the patristic dogma of the Holy Trinity and in the developed doctrine of Man) of monarchy, patriarchy and hierarchy.

So it is not surprising that wherever the ordination of women is accepted by a Church (e.g., ECUSA), other innovations or developments quickly follow, as modern ideologies compete to fill the space created by the dismissal of the principles of monarchy, patriarchy and hierarchy. These ideologies, dressed in the language of deity, not only fill the vacated space but also seek to take over completely the foundational thinking and the agenda of the Church.

But to take one step backwards, before the ordination of women can become a viable option for a Church, there has to have been both an erosion of biblical authority and a movement away from the classic dogma of the Trinity towards some other doctrine of God (e.g., panentheism) as a plurality in unity and unity in plurality (for these options see Peter Toon, *Our Triune God*). Usually there has also to be the influence of one or more modern ideologies (e.g., that of feminism).

Once women's ordination has arrived and is accepted by a Church, and thus the rejection of divine order has occurred, the life of the Church will inevitably progress into disorder—that is, will move further away from godly order and become more in tune with modern ideologies. As this occurs the Church, by secular standards, may seem to be "successful" and "useful" in society. However, the disorder will be apparent in such things as the adoption of inclusive language for Man and God, the movement into Pantheism or Panentheism, and major changes in the order, structure and language of Liturgy.

Further, the development of marriage services for homosexual persons who are living in what they call "faithful relationships" will occur and it will be common to ordain persons who are living in these "faithful relationships." By these developments there will be a total rejection of the doctrine of "one flesh" and the rejection of divine order in human relations. And by this time the Church will persecute those who still proclaim the biblical principles of monarchy, patriarchy and hierarchy! Further, the "community worship" of this Church will lack the majestic sense of the presence of the Holy LORD, for absent will be that "fear of the Lord" which is the beginning of both wisdom and knowledge!

Therefore, it may be claimed that while the doctrine of the sacrament of order is not the most important of Christian doctrines, it is a pivotal doctrine. To reject it is in fact to reject, in principle if not in practice, the primary doctrines concerning the Holy Trinity and the Person of Christ. To reject it is to open the window through which will blow the winds of secularist modernity. To set it aside is to ensure that apostasy will occur sooner or later.

So we end where we began in the Introduction of this book, celebrating Paul's teaching on order in I Corinthians 11. The HEAD of every man is Christ. The HEAD of a woman is her husband. The HEAD of Christ (Incarnate Word and Son of the Father) is God, the Father. And woman (pre-eminently in the history of salvation, the Virgin Mary) is the GLORY of man. In the Sacrament of Order this biblical order is maintained for the salvation of the world and as part of the new creation.

# Appendices
# and
# Bibliography

# APPENDIX I

# The Trinity and the Blessed Virgin Mary

Teaching about Mary, the mother of Jesus, has always performed the function of clarifying the Person of Jesus the Christ—along with his identity and saving work. Against the heretic Nestorius, the Council of Ephesus (431) said that Mary was Theotokos, the Mother of God. This teaching was repeated by the Council of Chalcedon (451) which also set forth the doctrine of Christ as One Person made known in two Natures.

To assert that the Lord Jesus Christ is One Person of Two Natures is also to say that Mary is the ever-virgin bride of the Most High. For, as St. Luke tells us, the Holy Spirit came upon her and "the power of the Most High overshadowed her" so that she is the "bride unwedded," the virgin bride and mother. The Son of God, the Second person of the Blessed, Holy and Undivided Trinity, assumed his manhood in the womb of the ever-virgin bride of the Most High.

This doctrine of Mary as the virgin-bride is useful for pastoral as well as theological purposes—especially if one wants to indicate that the virgin is not someone who does not get any sensual "satisfaction," but is rather one who is true to a vocation ordered towards another.

Both man and woman are ordered towards one another, so that the pursuit of happiness is not the same as the pursuit of self-actualization, but is the finding and being found by another who will name and claim the gifts one has prepared (so the responsible youth seeks marriage, employment or a "religious" vocation rather than a life of sensuality and stimulation).

Virginity is also to be defined in relational terms. Mary is the Mother of that Person who is both flesh and spirit, God and Man. That Person, however, is neither simply a human person nor a pre-existent soul, which takes a body. Also that Person is not a human subject in which divine and human being subsist.

The name Jesus, considered as the name of a personal subject, belongs to the Second Person of the Holy Trinity, the Son of God begotten before all ages, who is the Word of God, who is with God and who is God, through whom all things are made, and who for us and for our salvation became Man.

Mary, therefore, as the Mother of Jesus, is held to be Lady and Queen of all creation and of every creature. *She has a special relation of order to the Father and to the Son and to the Holy Spirit, and also to all creation.*

As the Antiphon to the Magnificat in the Divine Liturgy of the Orthodox Churches declares:

**O higher than the cherubim, incomparably more glorious than the seraphim; Blessed Lady and Queen, chosen Bride of the Most High, and ever-virgin Mother of God: Holy Mary, pray for us.**

# APPENDIX II

# The Trinity and Homosexuality

## MALE WITH MALE AND FEMALE WITH FEMALE CANNOT BE ONE FLESH

Within the main-line denominations of America there is a growing readiness to believe, teach and confess a new doctrine of marriage. That is, marriage is "a faithful relationship between two persons"—between a man and a man or between a woman and a woman or between a man and a woman.

At the General Convention of the Episcopal Church in 1994, over fifty bishops signed a statement entitled "Koinonia," written by Bishop Spong of Newark. This stated:

> We believe that sex is a gift of God. We believe that some of us are created heterosexual and some of us are created homosexual. We believe that both homosexuality and heterosexuality are morally neutral, that both can be lived out with beauty, honor, holiness, and integrity and that both are capable of being lived out destructively....

> We believe that those who know themselves to be gay
> or lesbian persons, and who do not choose to live alone,
> but forge relationships with partners of their choice
> that are faithful, monogamous, committed, life-giv-
> ing and holy are to be honored.

The basic premise of "Koinonia" is that one's sex is accidental (like the color of eyes or hair) and what is primary in marriage is a "faithful relationship." In contrast, in Genesis 2:23-24, we find that marriage is presented in terms of "one flesh," a unique relation of a man and a woman; "Therefore a man leaves his father and his mother and cleaves to his wife, and they become one flesh".

The Lord Jesus Christ accepted this fundamental teaching and added to it the words: "So they are no longer two but one. What, therefore, God has joined together, let no man put asunder" (Matt. 19:4-5).

For Jews and Christians it once went without question that "one flesh" could only be a union of male and female, whose bodies are designed by God to be united in coitus. Of course, "one flesh" is a union of hearts as well as bodies—as Paul declares in Ephesians 5:21—but this unique union necessarily includes the union of bodies for the purpose of procreation. It may be said that there is an ordered relation, designed by the Creator, between man and wife, and this relation which is marriage hopefully realizes a relationship of love and mutual respect. But the primary and fundamental reality is the ordered relation, which exists even when, for a time, there is no happy relationship!

What is clearly implied in the teaching of "one flesh" is also suggested by the doctrine that human beings ("Man") are made in the image and after the likeness of God. In Genesis we read; "So God created man in his own image, in the image of God he created him; male and female he created them (Gen. 1:27), and when God created man, he made him in the likeness of God. Male and female he created them and named them Man when they were created (Gen. 5:1-2).

While each and every human being is certainly made in the image and after the likeness of God, it would appear that the conjugal union of male and female reflects this image more clearly.

There is order within the Holy Trinity—the Father, the only begotten Son of the Father and the Holy Spirit, who proceeds from the Father. These three equal Persons in ordered relations, who are one God, one Deity, because each Person possesses wholly the one identical Godhead as do the other two Persons. However, in the Unity in Trinity and Trinity in Unity there is Order, for there are ordered relations between the Persons and these relations originate with the Father.

There is also order within the Holy Trinity's plan for the creation—man and then woman, two equal persons in an ordered relation, united as one flesh. Thus, the human race in its ordered relations and unity, expressed in marriage, reflects the plurality and unity of the living God. So it is not surprising that Jesus declared: "What God has joined together let no man put asunder."

Of course, God's plan for the human race also necessarily includes the relation of parents and children together with the complex relations of the family—thus, for example, the command to honor one's parents.

What God's plan does not include is the sexual union of man and beast, of man with man or of woman with woman. In fact, these possibilities are specifically excluded and declared to be sinful, as also is the breaking of the "one flesh" through fornication and adultery.

It is obvious that physical, sexual activity between two males, or two females, or a human being and an animal, cannot in any way be a reflection of the image and after the likeness of God. Certainly there can be and ought to be friendship between people of the same sex as also there can be and ought to be a close bond between human beings and animals. But there ought not to be sexual intimacies, and there cannot be genuine marriage between persons of the same sex, simply because they are not designed that way by God. The Lord made man as "male and female" not as "male and male" or "female and female." In short, two persons of the same sex cannot be one flesh, and it cannot be said of any such "faithful relationships" that "what God has joined together let no man put asunder."

**NOTE**

It has become common in modern English to use "gender" and "sex" as synonyms. This probably reflects a victory for those who wish to set aside the Judaeo-Christian traditions concerning the identity and nature of "sex." As Professor Peter L.Berger explains:

> "Gender" is feminist English for "sex." The very term reveals the ideological agenda. It is a term derived from grammar, unlike "sex," which refers (in this instance) to undeniable biological differences. Grammatical gender is freely variable. Thus the word for "sun" is feminine in German *(die Sonne)* and masculine in French *(le soleil)*; these gender assignments are arbitrary and could just as well be reversed. The ideological implication, of course, is that all so-called "gender roles" are just as freely variable—men nurturing babies, women ramming bayonets into enemy bellies, and so on. Comparative anthropological studies do show that the social roles assigned to the two sexes are variable to some extent. The notion, though, that these role assignments are sovereignly free of all biological determinants is almost certainly an illusion. (*First Things,* June 1996, vol. 64, p.19.)

To say that male and female are only different in gender and not sexually different is to establish a foundation upon which arguments in favor of "same-gender marriage" can be made. The use of correct terminology is important for the stating of right doctrine.

# APPENDIX III

# *ORDINATIO SACERDOTALIS*

## THE APOSTOLIC LETTER OF POPE JOHN PAUL II ON RESERVING PRIESTLY ORDINATION TO MAN ALONE

[The Bishop of Rome, Pope John Paul II, has a special affection for the Anglican Communion of Churches and was deeply grieved in 1994 when the Church of England decided to ordain women as priests. "*Ordinatio Sacerdotalis*" was written both in response to this event and because of calls from within the Catholic Church for the ordination of women.]

**1.** Priestly ordination, which hands on the office entrusted by Christ to his Apostles of teaching, sanctifying and governing the faithful, has in the Catholic Church from the beginning always been reserved to men alone. This tradition has also been faithfully maintained by the Oriental [Eastern] Churches.

When the question of the ordination of women arose in the Anglican Communion, Pope Paul VI, out of fidelity to his office of safeguarding the Apostolic Tradition, and also with a view to removing a new obstacle placed in the way of Christian unity, reminded Anglicans of the position of the Catholic Church: "She holds that it is not admissible to ordain women to the priesthood, for very fundamental reasons. These reasons include: the example recorded in the Sacred Scriptures of Christ choosing the Apostles only from among men; the constant practice of the Church which has imitated Christ in choosing only men; and her living teaching authority, which has consistently held that the exclusion of women from the priesthood is in accordance with God's plan for the Church" (*Response to Archbishop Donald Coggan*, Nov. 30, 1975).

But since the question had also become the subject of debate among theologians and in certain Catholic circles, Paul VI directed the Congregation of the Faith to set forth and expound the teaching of the Church on this matter. This was done through the Declaration, *Inter Insigniores*, which the supreme Pontiff approved and ordered to be published on October 15, 1976.

**2.** The Declaration recalls and explains the fundamental reasons for this teaching, reasons expounded by Paul VI, and concludes that the Church "does not consider herself authorized to admit women to priestly ordination." To these fundamental reasons the document adds other theological reasons which illustrate the appropriateness of the divine provision, and it also shows that Christ's way of acting did not proceed from sociological or cultural motives peculiar to his time. As Paul VI later explained: "The real reason is that, in giving the Church her fundamental constitution, her theological anthropology—thereafter always followed by the Church's tradition—Christ established things in this way" (*Insegnamenti*, XV, 1977, p.111).

In the Apostolic Letter, *Mulieris Dignitatem*, of August 15, 1988, I myself wrote: "In calling only men as his Apostles, Christ acted in a completely free and sovereign manner. In doing so, he exercised the same freedom with which, in all his behavior, he emphasized the dignity and vocation of women, without conforming to the prevailing customs and to the traditions sanctioned by the legislation of that time."

In fact, the Gospels and the Acts of the Apostles attest that this call was made in accordance with God's eternal plan: Christ chose those whom he willed (cf. Mark 3:13-14; John 6:70), and he did so in union with the Father through the Holy Spirit, after having spent the night in prayer (cf. Luke 6:12). Therefore, in granting admission to the ministerial priesthood, the Church has always acknowledged as a perennial norm her Lord's way of acting in choosing twelve men whom he made the foundation of his Church (cf. Rev. 21:24).

These men did not in fact receive only a function which could thereafter be exercised by any member of the Church; rather, they were specifically and intimately associated in the mission of the Incarnate Word himself (cf. Matt. 10:1, 7-8; 28:16-20; Mark 3:13-16; 16:14-15). The Apostles did the same when they chose fellow workers who would succeed them in their ministry. Also included in this choice were those who, throughout the time of the Church, would carry on the Apostles' mission of representing Christ the Lord and Redeemer.

**3.** Furthermore, the fact that the Blessed Virgin Mary, Mother of God and Mother of the Church, received neither the mission proper to the Apostles nor the ministerial priesthood clearly shows that the non-admission of women to priestly ordination cannot mean that women are of lesser dignity, nor can it be construed as discrimination against them. Rather, it is to be seen as the faithful observance of a plan to be ascribed to the wisdom of the Lord of the universe.

The presence and the role of women in the life and mission of the Church, although not linked to the ministerial priesthood, remains absolutely necessary and irreplaceable. As the Declaration, *Inter Insigniores* points out, "the Church desires that Christian women should become fully aware of the greatness of their mission: today their role is of capital importance both for the renewal and humanization of society and for the rediscovery by believers of the true face of the Church."

The New Testament and the whole history of the Church give ample evidence of the presence in the Church of women, true disciples, witnesses to Christ in the family and in society, as well as to total consecration to the service of God and the Gospel. "By defending the dignity of women and their vocation, the Church has shown honor and gratitude for those women who—faithful to the Gospel—have shared in every age in the apostolic mission of the whole People of God. They are the holy martyrs, virgins, and the mothers of families, who bravely bore witness to their faith and passed on the Church's faith and tradition by bringing up their children in the spirit of the Gospel" (*Mulieris Dignitatem*, 27).

Moreover, it is to the holiness of the faithful that the hierarchical structure of the Church is totally ordered. For this reason, the Declaration, *Inter Insigniores* recalls: "the only better gift, which can and must be desired, is love (cf. I Cor. 12 & 13). The greatest in the kingdom of heaven are not the ministers but the saints."

**4.** Although the teaching that priestly ordination is to be reserved to men alone has been preserved by the constant and universal Tradition of the Church and firmly taught by the Magisterium in its more recent documents, at the present time in some places it is nonetheless considered still open to debate, or the Church's judgment that women are not to be admitted to ordination is considered to have a merely disciplinary force.

> Wherefore, in order that all doubt may be removed regarding a matter of great importance, a matter which pertains to the Church's divine constitution itself, in virtue of my ministry of confirming the brethren (cf. Luke 22:32), I declare that the Church has no authority whatsoever to confer priestly ordination on women and that this judgment is to be definitively held by all the Church's faithful.

Invoking an abundance of divine assistance upon you, venerable Brothers, and upon the faithful. I impart my Apostolic Blessing.

From the Vatican, on May 22, the Solemnity of Pentecost, in the year 1994, the sixteenth of my Pontificate.

*Joannes Paulus II.*

# Notes

### Introduction
[1] Mary Daly, *Beyond God the Father: Toward a Philosophy of Women's Liberation* (Boston: Beacon Press, 1973), p. 19.

### Chapter 1
[1] Matt. 4:17-22; Mark 1:14-20; Luke 4:38-5:11; John 1:35-42.
[2] Luke 9:1-6, 10:1-22; Mark 6:7-13; Matt. 10:1-12; John 20:21-33.
[3] I.e., that of the 1979 Prayer Book of the ECUSA.
[4] Thomas Aquinas, *Summa Theologica*, Supplement Q92, Article 1.
[5] *Apostolic Constitutions*, Book III Section 1, ix, x, xi.
[6] Thomas Aquinas, *Summa Theologica*, Supplement: Article 1, reply to objection 3.

### Chapter 2
[1] As indicated by the various versions and interpretations of the Greek and Hebrew text of Deuteronomy 32:8.
[2] Daniel 7:14; Luke 1:33; cf. Matt. 26:63-64; Mark 14:61-62; Luke 22:66-71.
[3] *Mishnah,* 'kiddushin' 1.1.

### Chapter 5
[1] Cf. I Cor. 11:1-6; 14:33-40; Gal. 3:26-29; Eph. 5:21.
[2] Athanasius, *On the Incarnation*, LIV.
[3] Augustine, *On The Trinity*, Book VII, Chapter 4. There is an excellent discussion of the doctrine of relations in the dogma of

the Trinity in Jean Galot, *The Person of Christ* (Chicago: Franciscan Herald Press, 1983), pp. 25ff.

[4] By adding the *Filioque* clause to the Ecumenical or Nicene Creed, asserting that the Holy Spirit proceeds both from the Father "and the Son" the Western (Latin) Church has caused much grief. This clause might be taken to mean that the Spirit proceeds from the Father and the Son in such a way that the three Persons are defined by their "economic" relations in one divine nature, as "will" might be said to proceed from "memory" and "intellect," or "loving" might be said to proceed from "being" and "knowing." Such an approach would be to make the Persons functions or operations of one divine nature, which is the "God" to which we pray. Another possibility is that the *Filioque* clause might be taken to mean that the Spirit proceeds from the Father and the Son as a Child from a Father and Mother, making the Son of God into the Wife of God, and Mother of the Spirit of God. Then also the ordered relations of memory, intellect and will can be used to show that the same form may subsist in three related ways. The ordered relations of Adam, Seth and Eve can be used to show that three persons may be distinguished according to their manner of coming to be, without any reference to nature or attribute, but only to relations (Adam is made, Seth is begotten of Adam, and Eve proceeds from Adam without conceptual reference to time, space, nature or sexual process; so the Father is uncreated and unoriginate, the Son is begotten of the Father, and the Holy Spirit proceeds from the Father). But such illustrations of ordered relations are given without reference to the Filioque. The addition of the *Filioque* tends to confuse the economic and interpersonal relations of the Trinity. Jesus pours out the Spirit on us, because he gives us what the Father has given him, not because he is a cause of the Spirit's coming to be. This sort of distinction between the sending and the procession of the Spirit is made in Scripture even more clearly than in the Ecumenical Creed defined by the Council of Constantinople I (381). "But when the Counselor comes, whom I shall send to you from the Father, even the Spirit of truth, who proceeds from the Father, he will bear witness to me...." (John 15:26).

134

[5] From the Orthodox Troparion for the Vespers of Pentecost; see Isabel Florence Hapgood, *Service Book of The Holy Orthodox Catholic Apostolic Church* (Englewood; NJ: 1983; cf. John 1:32-33). See further, Peter Toon, *Our Triune God: A Biblical Portrayal of the Trinity* (Wheaton, IL: Victor Books, 1996) and *Yesterday, Today and Forever: Jesus Christ and the Holy Trinity in the Teaching of the Seven Ecumenical Councils* (Swedesboro, NJ: Preservation Press, 1996).

## Chapter 7

[1] Cf. Plato, *Symposium* and Hesiod *The Works and Days/Theogeny.*

[2] Cf. Thomas Aquinas, *Summa Theologica*, Pt. 1, Q21 Art. 1 reply to objection 3.

[3] At the back of *The Book of Common Prayer* (1662), there is a Table of Persons, related by Consanguinity and Affinity, whom one may or may not marry.

[4] Cf. Michael P. Jones, *Degenerate Moderns: Modernity as Rationalized Sexual Misbehaviour* (San Francisco: Ignatius Press, 1993) and *Dionysos Rising: The Birth of Cultural Revolution out of The Spirit of Music* (San Francisco: Ignatius Press, 1994).

[5] The revision of theology has already been noted in the shift from a consideration of the Fatherhood of God from the Sonship of Christ to a consideration from the Brotherhood of Man. The revision of Scripture as prayed can be seen in the 1979 Book of Common Prayer's revision of the Psalms. In Psalm 1:1 "blessed is the man" is replaced by "blessed are they" (putting a plural for a singular, and a neuter for a masculine form). In Psalm 51:5/6 "in sin hath my mother conceived me" is replaced by "I have been a sinner from my mother's womb." The orders of consanguinity and affinity are both revised out of the text for the sake of a sexless individuality. The same mentality can be seen in the New Revised Standard Version of the Bible, which with other "new" versions employs politically correct "inclusive" language, based on the ideologies of individualism, humanism and nationalism, in order to avoid politically incorrect "exclusive" language, based on the order of

generation and marriage. In the Book of the Prophet Ezekiel, the term "Son of Man" is replaced by the term "Mortal," thus replacing a term interpreted not only by the prophetic ministry of Ezekiel but also the vision of Daniel, the statements of our Lord with respect to his own passion/exaltation, and the martyr's vision of St. Stephen, with a term shaped by the philosopher and apparently political fascist Martin Heidegger to speak of human self consciousness as a consciousness of impending death and our present mortality in contrast with immortality. In this philosophy we are not made for likeness with God, so that we face his Reality and judgment; rather, we are "thrown into the world" towards death and the grave. It may be said that a different religion is being promoted by the ideological revision of theology and Scripture.

### Chapter 8

[1] Thomas Aquinas, *Summa Theologica*, Pt. 1, Q47, Art. 3.
[2] "The Form of The Solemnization of Matrimony," in the *Book of Common Prayer* (1662).
[3] For "image and likeness" see Gen. 1:26f, 5:1ff; Lev. 19:1; Matt. 5:48; Luke 6:36. For "son of God" see Luke 3:38; I Chron. 28:6, Hosea 11:1. For "bridegroom" see Hosea 2:16-20; Ez. 16: John 3:29; Matt. 9:15; Mark 2:19; Luke 5:34.
[4] Cf. Gen. 2:23, 29:14; II Sam. 5:1, 19:12; I Cor. 11:3, 12:12-30; Rom. 12:4-8; Eph. 5:21-33.
[5] See the Greek of I Cor. 11:7.
[6] Of the sin of the Angel of Babylon and the Angel of Tyre in Ezekiel 28:1-19; and Isaiah 14:12-15.
[7] I Cor. 14:37; see the discussion of the "command of the Lord" in Manfred Hauke, *Women In The Priesthood? A Systematic Analysis in the light of the Order of Creation and Redemption* (San Francisco: Ignatius Press, 1988).

### Chapter 9

[1] In the *Mishnah*, the man sanctifies the woman to himself by a gift. "Kiddushin" 1.1.
[2] Psalm 8:4-5; Gal. 3:19-4:9; Luke 20:36; Heb. 1:1-14.

## Chapter 10

[1] For the text see St. Luke's Journal of Theology, June, 1988, p. 180.

[2] See further, W. M. Hardenbrook, *Missing from Action: Vanishing Manhood in America* (Nashville: Thomas Nelson, 1987), p. 138.

[3] See Appendix III or the Apostolic Letter *Ordinatio Sacerdotalis* by Pope John Paul II, "On Reserving Priestly Ordination to Men Alone" (22 March 1994).

[4] *Catechism of the Catholic Church.* (1994), par. 1537.

[5] Thomas Aquinas, *Summa Theologica*, Supplement, Q39, Art. 1.

[6] *Ibid.*, Supplement Q39, Art. 1.

[7] *Ibid.*, Pt. 1, Q92, Art. 1. See also Hauke, *op. cit., p. 207.*

[8] Hauke, *op. sit., p. 207.*

[9] Thomas Aquinas, *Summa theologica*, Supplement Q40, Art. 5.

[10] *Apostolic Constitutions*, Book III, Section iv.

[11] *Ibid.,* Section ii.

[12] *Ibid.*, Sec. i, ix, x, xi.

[13] Ignatius of Antioch, *Epistle to the Trallians*, III, 1.

[14] *Apostolic Constitutions*, Book II, Section xxvi; Book II, Section iv.

## Chapter 11

[1] Gregory Nazianzen, *First Theological Oration.*

[2] Such a doctrine of God is in fact proposed by the Standing Liturgical Commission of the Episcopal Church in one of its eucharistic prayers for Prayer Book Studies 30. God is said to have prepared the world before the creation, and then to have given birth to all things. Such teaching is panentheism.

[3] Joseph Hertz, *The Authorized Daily Prayer Book* (Hebrew and English), "Morning Service Preliminaries" (New York: Bloch Publishing, 1974), p. 51.

# Select Bibliography

*Ante-Nicene Fathers.* Vol. 7, *Apostolic Constitutions.* New York: Christian Literature Company, 1886; reprint ed., Peabody, MA: Hendrickson Publishers, Inc., 1994.

Athanasius, St. *On the Incarnation,* ed. R. W. Thomson. *Oxford Early Christian Texts.* Oxford: Oxford University Press, 1971.

Augustine, St. *On the Trinity.* Vol. 3, *The Nicene and Post-Nicene Fathers.* First Series. New York: Christian Literature Company, 1887; reprint ed., Peabody, MA: Hendrickson Publishers, Inc., 1994.

*Book of Common Prayer (1662).* London: Oxford University Press, 1990.

*Book of Common Prayer of the Episcopal Church, USA (1979).* New York: Episcopal Church, 1979.

*Catechism of the Catholic Church.* San Francisco: Ignatius Press, 1994.

Daly, Mary. *Beyond God the Father.* Boston: Beacon Press, 1973.

Galot, Jean, S.J. *The Person of Christ: A Theological Insight.* Chicago: Franciscan Herald Press, 1983.

Gregory of Nazianzus, St. *Five Theological Orations*, ed. A. J. Mason. Cambridge: Cambridge Patristic Texts, 1899.

Hauke, Manfred. *Women in the Priesthood? A Systematic Analysis in the Light of the Order of Creation and Redemption.* San Francisco: Ignatius Press, 1988.

Jones, Michael. *Degenerate Moderns: Modernity as Rationalized Sexual Misbehaviour.* San Francisco: Ignatius Press, 1993.

Kroeger, C. C. "Head" in *Dictionary of Paul and his Letters.* ed. Gerald F. Hawthorne. Downers Grove, Illinois: Intervarsity Press, 1993: pp. 375-378.

*Service Book of the Holy Orthodox Catholic Apostolic Church.* trans. Florence Hapgood. Englewood, N.J.: 1983.

Tanner, N. F. ed. *Decrees of the Ecumenical Councils.* 2 vols. London and Washington, D.C.: Georgetown University Press, 1990.

Thomas Aquinas, St. *Summa Theologica.* London, Eyre & Spottiswood, 1960ff. Blackfriars edition.

Toon, Peter. *Our Triune God: A Biblical Portryal of the Trinity.* Wheaton, IL: Victor Books, 1996.

Toon, Peter. *Yesterday, Today and Forever: Jesus Christ and the Holy Trinity in the Teaching of the Seven Ecumenical Councils.* Swedesboro, N.J.: Preservation Press, 1996.